A DOG
IN THE CAVE

The Wolves Who Made Us Human

Kay Frydenborg

Houghton Mifflin Harcourt
Boston   New York

www.hmhco.com

Photo credits can be found on page 241.

Book design by Rebecca Bond

The text of this book is set in Adobe Caslon Pro

The Library of Congress Cataloging-in-Publication data is on file.

ISBN: 978-0-544-28656-6

Printed in China

SCP 10 9 8 7 6 5 4 3 2 1

4500635247

CONTENTS

When the Man waked up he said, "What is Wild Dog doing here?"
And the Woman said, "His name is not Wild Dog any more,
but the First Friend, because he will be our friend for always
and always and always."

Rudyard Kipling
"The Cat That Walked by Himself"
Just So Stories

It is scarcely possible to doubt that the love of man
has become instinctive in the dog.

Charles Darwin
On the Origin of Species

A BOY AND HIS DOG

This Siberian husky may closely resemble the earliest dogs of Paleolithic Eurasia, based on current fossil and genetic evidence. Scientists believe these dogs would have been somewhat larger than this modern dog, more similar in size to a large German shepherd.

A boy walks barefoot into a large, multichambered cave in what is now southern France, pausing a moment just inside for his eyes to adjust from daylight to darkness. Deep within the cave it's black as night, so he carries a torch made of long-burning juniper pitch to light his way. Lifting it just above eye level, he stops periodically to examine the elaborate display of artwork lining the cave walls around him.

The paintings seem more than merely decorative. They're intense and remarkably accurate, depicting a single, urgent subject: large animals. In the flickering light cast by the young boy's torch parades a menagerie of ancient wild beasts, frozen in time, arrayed across a rough canvas of limestone. At least thirteen different species are captured in dynamic, lifelike poses, painted and etched into rock by human hands at least five thousand years before the boy's time. It's the oldest collection of representational art ever discovered in the world, which many scholars believe signals the beginnings of a modern human consciousness. But the boy knows nothing of that.

A panel of rhinos painted by early humans on the walls of Chauvet Cave some 31,000 years ago.

And the panel of lions.

Is he looking for something in particular on this day? Some crucial bit of information, perhaps, encoded in the silent forms of horses, mammoths, cave lions, and bears? Does he step closer to trace, with the tip of his finger, the long, upwardly curving horn of a rhinoceros or the fixed stare of a massive cave bear? Does he, perhaps, sniff the dank air of the cave for the alarming scent of bear, or listen for the muffled breath of some other fearsome predator crouching just around the next dark corner?

Here he scrapes his torch against the rock wall to knock off spent ash and regenerate the flame, and perhaps to mark his way back out to light and air. Maybe he's entered this cave once before with other members of his clan, but today he's come without

The Pont d'Arc is a large natural bridge in the Ardeche district of southern France, a short distance from both Chauvet Cave and the town of Vallon-Pont-d'Arc. It has spanned the Ardeche River for about 500,000 years. Today a popular canoeing and kayaking destination for tourists, it's usually described as the natural entrance to the Ardeche Canyon, and would have been a well-traveled path for the humans who inhabited the area as long as 32,000 years ago.

the others, in pursuit of some adventure or ritual we can only imagine.

But he's not really alone. For next to the child strides a large, wolflike dog. Their footprints, fossilized in long-undisturbed mud of the cave floor, reveal that the boy is about eight or ten years old, four and a half feet tall. And the unusual animal by his side is easily as big as a wolf, with a paw the size of a grown man's hand. But those paw prints could have been left only by an animal that was neither a fully wild wolf nor a truly domesticated dog. It's an in-between beast we could call a wolf-dog.

The residue left behind by the child's torch rubbings tells us that the boy and his dog arrived at this back chamber of Chauvet Cave some twenty-six thousand years ago—more than seventeen thousand years earlier than the previously accepted date of the earliest human domestication of gray wolves, the ancestors of all modern dogs. Yet there it is, unmistakable evidence that a dog walked there that long ago.

The boy and dog may have been the very last to enter this particular cave for thousands of years. Its entrance was blocked by a rock collapse soon after their visit, and it very likely remained sealed until 1994. That was when three local cavers happened upon it and, entering by way of an alternate entrance, discovered a hidden treasure that rocked the world.

I

CLOSE ENCOUNTERS
OF THE CANINE KIND

A search dog named Ben leaps exhuberantly in a moment of play.

hen first reported in 1994, the tracks of the wolf-like dog in Chauvet Cave—featuring a shortened middle toe that only dogs, and not wolves, possess—were dismissed by most scientists. Evidence for the existence of such an animal in prehistory radically differed from the then-known fossil record, contradicting accepted theories of dog domestication. Before the Chauvet Cave discovery, most scientists dated the earliest domestication of dogs to about twelve thousand years ago, based largely on a 1977 archaeological find in northern Israel. There, buried under the floor of an ancient dwelling, lay the skeletons of an elderly human and a four-month-old puppy. The human's hand was found resting gently on the dog's chest. This was thought to be the earliest known evidence of the enduring domestic relationship between human and dog.

But 1977 is ancient history in the fast-moving field of dog science. New evidence is drastically reshaping how scientists understand the origins and shared history of human beings and dogs and is revealing a deeper and more complex connection between our two species than even the dog lovers among us had ever imagined. The more we learn about dogs, the more it appears that our species' relationship with them may have begun as one of cooperation, rather than one of dominance and submission—a true partnership going all the way back to the earliest meetings of humans and certain rather unusual wolves.

This is *not* the way humans have long thought about the animals we've domesticated, and about ourselves as godlike creators, shaping other species through deliberate selective breeding. But dogs are not like any other domesticated animals. Humans and dogs have traveled so closely together through time that both we and our dogs have been profoundly changed in fundamental ways: how we relate to others, how we think and process information, how we act, and even how our bodies look and work. Many scientists consider this a prime example of *coevolution*, a process by which two species sharing a similar environment evolve in a kind of dance, with changes in one species triggering related changes in the other over time. If these mutual changes provide a survival and reproductive advantage—as happened with one special group of wolves who, for whatever reason, became associated with humans—genetic mutations are passed down in succeeding generations and become permanent features.

New discoveries in paleontology and genetics locate the beginnings of our partnership with dogs at a much earlier time in our evolutionary history than once believed, suggesting that the development of social cooperation among humans might coincide with the beginning of ancient humans' collaborative hunting with dogs. Though there's no clear proof yet that one development directly caused the other, mounting evidence has led many anthropologists and evolutionary biologists to suggest that wolves-turned-dogs played a fundamental role in "domesticating" early humans just as we domesticated them. Many scientists studying our evolutionary history now believe that social cooperation among early humans and collaborative hunting with dogs may be directly related.

It seems clear that social cooperation is the key behavior programmed into our species that allowed humankind to dominate the animal kingdom and radically reshape our world, but it was quite an evolutionary leap. Humans are, after all, a species of primate most closely related to chimpanzees, an animal described in this way by the renowned primatologist Jane Goodall:

Unlike wolves, chimpanzees (the species most closely related to humans) are contentious and volatile by nature, often settling disputes with physical aggression.

"Chimpanzees are individualists. They are boisterous and volatile in the wild. They are always on the lookout for ways to get the better of each other. They are not pack animals."

Gray wolves, on the other hand, are the quintessential pack animals. The top predator of Ice Age Europe and Asia despite extremely challenging environmental conditions, the gray wolf succeeded precisely because of its cooperative social structure. Like modern wolves, ancient wolves ran down prey in well-organized teams, helped one another to carry and guard the kill, provided cooperatively for the young of their pack, and delegated responsibilities such as protection, scouting, and babysitting in a way that resembles the organization of human societies today.

In the Ngorongoro Conservation Area of Tanzania, a Masai warrior walks across the African plains, returning from a successful day of hunting gazelle with his dog.

These social skills would have given wolves a distinct advantage over the earliest human hunters — still mostly solitary scavengers like their primate ancestors.

At some point, though, humans, too, learned to hunt in cooperative groups, and they became top predators, rivaling wolves. Scientists believe that when wolves first walked into human society, we developed an interspecies relationship based on a shared genetic predisposition to cooperate in a group—something that wolves had refined as a winning strategy for millions of years before it became hardwired into human nature.

Scientists from Charles Darwin to the eminent Harvard biologist E. O. Wilson have long pondered the equally powerful yet contradictory tendencies in human nature to strive individually ("survival of the fittest") and to cooperate with others, even to the point of sometimes altruistically sacrificing our own lives for the benefit of others.

Both the instinctive social cooperation that we share with wolves and dogs (and many other species) and the highly competitive nature that we share with most other members of the primate family are exemplified in today's cutting-edge dog

A small wolf pack together in winter.

A hunting pack of six wolves surrounds a bison on
a snowy day in Yellowstone National Park.

research—one of the most contentious but increasingly collaborative, creative, and rapidly evolving fields in modern science.

Most dog scientists now agree that the intimate relationship
that developed between two very different, but equally successful, species changed both humans and the wolves who became
the first dogs in profound ways. Many even believe that the idea
of coevolution between humans and dogs leads directly to a startling conclusion: without one another, neither humans nor dogs,
as we know them today, would exist. The dog truly *is* humankind's best friend—more profoundly like us, in surprising ways,
than any other species on earth.

HOW MANY DOGS?

Reliable population statistics for the world's dogs are hard to come by because most of them are anonymous and more or less fend for themselves. But it's hard to imagine a time *before* dogs were our partners and companions, since dogs are everywhere. Today, in the United States alone, more than 54 million households support an estimated dog population of up to 78 million. Worldwide, adding together all the rough estimates, at least 525 million dogs share our planet today. How many dogs is that? To get a sense of this figure, imagine the total number of people in the United States, Canada, Great Britain, Germany, Italy, and France—that's about how many dogs there are in the world.

If it's true that familiarity breeds contempt, the familiar, comforting presence of dogs in our midst has long bred scientific neglect, at best. Until recently domestic canines were of little interest to science; serious biological and cognitive scientists focused on humans, first and foremost, and next on wild animals, which together make up most of the animal kingdom. Of all the animal species alive in the world now or in the past, only a relatively few have been domesticated by humans, most of them in just the last few thousand years of human history. The dog was the first, by a wide margin—the only animal believed to have been domesticated by itinerant human hunter-gatherers, long before the development of farming and permanent settlements. And yet, for most of our shared history, the details of how this remarkable interspecies relationship developed have remained a mystery.

It wasn't until the very end of the twentieth century that a few scientists began to investigate the unique relationship between dogs and humans. A handful of evolutionary biologists and cognitive scientists led the way, and their surprising discoveries would soon open the floodgates of groundbreaking dog-centered research. In less than twenty years, dog science—a field that had barely existed before—would begin to seem almost crowded. Scientists from many diverse fields—archaeology, anthropology, genetics, zoology, psychology, and ethology—would, in the next few years, undertake investigations of the deep bond between humans and dogs, born of our shared evolutionary, biological, and cultural past.

But long before scientists started to develop new tools to understand how, when, and where wolves were transformed into dogs, writers and artists throughout history, and all over the world, had been telling the remarkable story of dogs and humans, together through time.

The footprints in Chauvet Cave are like a snapshot in time—from far, far back—raising many more questions than have yet been answered. It's not even certain that the tracks mean what we want to think they mean: that a protodog and Paleolithic boy walked together through the ancient cave at the same moment, as companions and fellow explorers. But scientists agree that *could* be the explanation, and the image of a boy exploring his world with a friendly dog makes perfect sense to us today. It almost seems to collapse thousands of years of our past, making the distant world of our Paleolithic ancestors real and easy to comprehend in that moment of suspended time.

If a dog walked beside a young boy in a French cave twenty-six thousand years ago, it happened thousands of years before written records were kept. Since the earliest known written texts date from some five thousand years ago, any quest to unravel the origins of our ancient, epic relationship with dogs begins with *un*written forms of communication. Representational art, like that found on the walls of Chauvet Cave, is the first kind of

In this neolithic rock art painted in the Libyan Sahara sometime between 5000 and 1000 B.C., sheep are pursued by two hunters with their three hunting dogs.

"text" available for analysis. Ancient fossils and artifacts provide a different sort of tangible record that paleontologists can follow back to the beginnings of modern humans and dogs. All such evidence is subject to interpretation and accurate dating, which means that "reading" fossils is always a work in progress.

Written descriptions and stories of dogs in various cultures throughout history provide a fascinating and sweeping view of dogs through time—but a view that leaves out the very earliest interactions between humans and dogs, which scientists now believe occurred long before human writing was invented and widely practiced. Fully developed writing systems appeared only with the transition from hunter-gatherer cultures to more permanent agricultural settlements when, for the first time, it became necessary to count property—from parcels of land to animals and measures of grain—or to transfer that property to another individual or another settlement.

But while dogs were certainly a part of everyday life for the first farmers, the literature of dogs began much later, perhaps with the *Epic of Gilgamesh,* set in ancient Mesopotamia and written from 2150 to 1400 B.C. In this great tale, seven hunting dogs appear as companions to the goddess Ishtar; in another famous story from the period, the husband of this popular goddess keeps his own domesticated dogs as part of his royal household. A different goddess, Gula, associated with health and healing, was often depicted in the presence of her dog. Dogs were widely thought to have healing powers; a belief in the "healing power" of dog saliva persists to this day, as does the phrase "licking one's wounds" to describe the process of recovering from injury or defeat in battle. But dogs were not just for the gods; they also featured prominently in Mesopotamian art depicting the everyday lives of ordinary people, where dogs were seen as companions, protectors of herds and houses, and all-around clean-up crews who removed dead animals and other refuse from village streets.

Only two main breeds are described in these early images and stories: large greyhounds used mostly for hunting and *very* large, strong dogs resembling the Great Danes and mastiffs of today, who protected both herds and humans from wild wolves and other dangers. Dogs were commonly kept in the home and loved by their human families, much as they are in many households today.

The same story was repeated in ancient Egypt, and continued throughout the time of classical Greek civilization. After the Roman Empire took over Greece in the Battle of Corinth in 146 B.C. and then greatly expanded to encompass vast territories in the Middle East, North Africa, and Europe, the Romans began deliberately crossing canines from all of these regions, creating more kinds of dogs than had ever existed before. There were now, besides mastiffs and greyhounds of all sizes, many different kinds of hounds, curly-coated poodle types, and tiny lapdogs whose only function was to be amusingly cute.

The Middle Ages were a dark time for humans and dogs alike, defined by wars, famine, superstition, and disease. Beginning in 1347, the bubonic plague, a deadly bacterium transmitted by fleas—carried on the backs of black rats that had traveled from Asia to Europe and

An Egyptian Anubis statue. Anubis, usually depicted as a dog or jackal, sometimes with the body of a man, was a god of the dead, whom he was believed to protect on their route to the afterlife.

the Mediterranean aboard merchant ships—overwhelmed the populations of Europe. In many regions mortality rose as high as 95 percent, wiping out entire families, from aristocrats to beggars, and killing people faster than they could be buried. Most domesticated animals—cattle, sheep, poultry, and even cats—were also devastated by the scourge. Dogs, long exposed to fleas, seemed to possess a limited natural immunity to the disease, but hundreds were left ownerless and homeless, reduced to scavenging the bodies of the dead to survive. Roving packs of desperate feral dogs added to the horror of the epidemic for humans who managed to survive. The sickness raged for fifty years, until it burned itself out. Famine and a near-total breakdown of civilized society ensued.

But some fortunate people—a social elite with money and connections—rode out the plague years by enjoying access to vast tracts of unspoiled forest land, precious stocks of food and medicinal plants, and other prime resources. With this privilege came both large amounts of leisure

A Roman mosaic of a dog, above the legend "Cave Canem" (Beware of the Dog), from first-century Pompeii, from the collection of Naples National Museum.

time and the trappings of wealth. Privileged gentlemen turned back to hunting, which for the first time was elevated to a sport for the idle few, rather than a means of survival for the common person.

The fourteenth century was the beginning of a golden age of dog breeding. Hunting became increasingly lavish, ritualized, and complex; large hunting dogs were prized, since they were essential to the success of the entire hunting enterprise. Tiny lapdogs, on the other hand, still lived luxuriously—as they had for centuries in the ancient world—as pampered status symbols for the rich, the royal, and the powerful.

By the sixteenth century, intensified interest in the different uses of dogs had produced several more canine types as dogs continued to drift farther away from their wolfish roots. Besides those bred for the original purposes of hunting and guarding, there now were specialized types of hounds: scenthounds with relatively short legs who could hunt through the woodlands of northern Europe with their noses to the ground, as well as the original sighthounds—greyhounds, salukis, and similar long-legged, fast-running dogs—originally developed for the open hunting vistas of Africa and the Middle East. There were bird dogs, easily trained to gently cradle a wounded bird in their mouth and bring it to the hunter intact, and smaller, scrappier terriers, bred to independently hunt vermin such as rats and badgers, as well as small game animals such as rabbits and foxes. There were shepherd dogs, raised from an early age around flocks of sheep or other livestock, who, through a combination of natural instinct, intelligence, and training, would herd and faithfully guard these adopted nonhuman charges.

By then dogs, having evolved in Europe and Asia for thousands of years, had changed a great deal since their earliest days. But were they also evolving in other parts of the world? For a long time, scientists wondered if dogs might have been originally domesticated in North America, in the vast expanses of land teeming with wolves. Gray wolves had coexisted with the even larger dire wolves on the American continent for four hundred thousand years before the first wave of human migrants arrived, and fossil evidence of domestic dogs in America had been discovered in the early twentieth century. But until modern genetic analysis could be applied to these fossils, no one could be sure of their origin. With genomic analysis, the broad outline of dogs in America began to emerge from the mists of time.

About fifteen to ten thousand years ago, when people crossed the strip of land known as the Bering Land Bridge, which then connected Siberia and Alaska, they brought their dogs with them. Without the dogs, these first Asian American immigrants might not have survived such an arduous journey. Their large dogs had become essential; they could have pulled and carried belongings and food and defended the travelers from predators;

and if necessary, some of them could have been eaten along the way.

Some of the first conclusive evidence of the presence of domestic dogs in America came in the form of frozen dog remains found by gold miners near Fairbanks, Alaska, in the 1920s. The bones were donated to the American Museum of Natural History in New York City, where they lay untouched for more than seventy years. It would be 2002 before an analysis of their DNA could begin to reveal how these dogs had gotten there.

The oldest evidence of domesticated dogs yet found in the Americas came from a cave in Texas. It suggests that by then, people there were breeding dogs for food, as well as for work, protection, and companionship. A small bone fragment discovered in the cave was identified as part of a dog's skull; it was inside some dried fecal remains from a 9,400-year-old human. The bone was small enough to pass through the human intestinal system, said the lead researcher, but it also suggested that people at the time perhaps didn't chew their food very well. Maybe they'd learned to "wolf" down their meals from their canine companions! Archaeologists believe some unknown group of hunter-gatherers occupied this cave at the time. From the size of the bone, researchers estimate that it came from a twenty-five- to thirty-pound dog that may have resembled some still existing breeds of Mexican and Peruvian dogs.

Native Americans, before their first contact with Europeans, kept three basic types of dogs. In the Alaskan Arctic, where the earliest American dogs had first set foot on the continent,

A Native American encampment depicted in an 1882 engraving. Several dogs can be seen resting in the foreground.

dogs retained their wolfish proportions, as Alaskan malamutes, huskies, and sled dogs still do today. But smaller dogs were kept by some Indian tribes farther south. Some were the size of foxes, and some even had webbed feet, making them excellent water dogs; they were used for hunting otters or driving fish into nets. In the Southwest, southern Mexico, South America, and the Caribbean, evidence of much smaller dogs was found. Their colors could have been black or brown, spotted, tawny, or in shades of gray. The most unusual of all may have been the slate or reddish-gray hairless dogs of Mexico, living among the Aztec and the people of coastal Peru. They came in miniature, small, and medium sizes, and were both widely traded and highly valued.

It's difficult to find native dogs or their descendants today. Only a few modern dog breeds in the Americas have survived with their original genetic makeup largely intact: Inuit sled dogs, Alaskan malamutes, and Greenland dogs in the north, as well as Chihuahuas, and Mexican and Peruvian hairless dogs in the south.

Between those two geographic borders, only one other group of dogs has ancient roots that have been confirmed. Known as the Carolina dog, it's a primitive, semiferal canine living in the southeastern United States that bears a striking resemblance to the Australian dingo or Asian village dog. Carolina dogs probably descended from domesticated dogs left behind by Cherokee tribespeople who were forced off their lands in the early 1800s. When that happened, scientists believe, abandoned dogs disappeared into the surrounding forests and lived in isolation until they were rediscovered by a University of Georgia research ecologist in the 1970s. Because they had had little contact with either people or other dogs over the years, their genetic inheritance wasn't much affected by interbreeding with other canines.

But beyond these few, most of the familiar dogs we know and love today in America did not exist five hundred years ago, and most of the American dogs of that day have vanished. Why?

Just over five hundred years ago, there were two worlds on our planet, and neither knew of the other's existence. Then they met, in a culture clash that dramatically reshaped the world of the first Americans and their dogs. From the time of Christopher

Columbus's second landing on the shores of what Europeans soon called the New World in October 1492, successive waves of Spanish conquerors pushed their way from the islands of the Caribbean to the shores of Mexico, across all of Central America, and eventually to the South American continent. These conquistadors came armed with advanced weaponry and horses, which gave them a lopsided advantage; they also brought with them their dogs of war.

These dogs were large and ferocious, bred and trained for warfare — specifically for chasing and dismembering Mesoamerican and South American Indians and, later, African slaves. Large numbers of such dogs had been used in warfare throughout Europe, from the late Middle Ages into the Renaissance.

The extreme brutality with which these dogs were employed against native people who stood in the way of conquest was eventually documented and opposed by a small group of Spanish Dominican priests who had followed the conquistadors on a mission to convert native people to Catholicism. Eventually, the Spanish imperial court put an end to the worst abuses against the Indians, although African slaves were not accorded the same protections until considerably later.

Within a few decades of that first European contact with Mesoamericans, as many as 90 percent of the original inhabitants of Central and South America had perished — murdered by Europeans and their war dogs or sickened by fatal diseases carried by the invaders, their dogs, and their domestic cattle, sheep, pigs, and goats, to which the Indians had no natural immunity.

Many Native American dogs also succumbed to disease, and most of the indigenous dog breeds who survived the onslaught gradually disappeared, their genetic heritage lost through interbreeding with the European dogs.

The Spanish conquest represented only the first of many waves of Europeans to spread out across America over the next several centuries. Native peoples and cultures of North America were largely obliterated, and so were their dogs.

Though they had never seen horses before the Europeans brought them, many Native Americans came to embrace horse culture and made it their own. They learned how to raise and herd livestock from Christian missionaries who arrived, once again, to replace their native cultures and religions. Spanish-bred mastiffs were also converted, from killers of men, women, and children to tender and talented guardians of sheep, their ferocity now directed at any wolves, bears, or marauding dogs that threatened their woolly charges. These dogs, too, were soon lost to American history with the defeat of the Navajo and Apache tribes in the late nineteenth century. The mastiffs were replaced by smaller sheepdogs trained according to traditional Spanish methods. By then, the descendants of the first Americans were often seen in the company of dogs who bore the unmistakable traits of their European lineage, sprung from the now-extinct Eurasian wolves whom we can only imagine today by looking at traces of their genetic material in modern dogs.

2
WRITTEN IN THE BONES

More than 190 cave bear skulls have been found in Chauvet Cave. One was placed very carefully on the edge of a block of stone for some unknown purpose.

Though dogs were very much a part of Native American culture, the fossil record strongly suggests their beginnings lie elsewhere. Pictures and stories are the earliest records of dogs and their place in human culture, but like all art, they're subjective, intriguing, and mysterious. Why are there no wolves among the many animal figures depicted on the walls of Chauvet Cave? Yet the bones of once-living wolves were scattered among those of cave bears and hyenas inside the cave, and the footprints of a transitional wolf-dog creature were found preserved on the cave's ancient mud floor along with those of a human boy.

What does it mean that the oldest cave paintings found in America so far, discovered in Tennessee's Cumberland Plateau and dating from six thousand years ago, include many images of wild canids, unlike the earlier cave art of Europe, which contains almost none?

And if the hunting dogs belonging to the goddess Ishtar in the epic tale *Gilgamesh* are mythological creatures, what can they tell us about real dogs living in the Middle East four thousand years ago? Even with more complete knowledge of the basic history of dogs since the time of ancient Greece, scientists attempting to trace the full history of dogs, their unique bond with humans, and their evolution from wolves needed more specific evidence, because there were so many unanswered questions!

How could Ice Age humans have domesticated a species at the very top of the food chain, dangerous, ferocious competitors, extremely possessive of their food, who consumed as much as eleven pounds of meat per wolf per day—the same meat that ancient humans needed to survive? How might early humans have conceived of such a risky plan? How could there have been any future to this relationship at all? It had never happened before in the world, and it has never happened again. *When* did it happen? And, for that matter, where?

Until quite recently, the answers to such questions relied solely on interpreting the shape and placement of fossils dug out of the earth, long buried under layers and layers of time, or hidden in remote caves all over the world. Working painstakingly over many years, archaeologists and paleontologists began to piece together a story revealed in the fossilized bones of early modern humans and of their fellow hominids, the often misunderstood Neanderthals; those of plant-eating prey animals they both hunted; and those of ancient wolves and the earliest dogs.

It was only in the late 1990s that modern genetics began to add dramatically to scientific understanding of our ancient past and of the animals with whom we shared it. Advances in brain imaging and cognitive science are beginning to shed new light on how the first domesticated animal thinks — and even on what our dogs think about *us* now. But questions of how this relationship began in the first place remain unsettled, with new studies appearing at a dizzying pace, each one seeming to contradict those preceding it. Still, there is general agreement on some findings.

Something most unusual must have occurred between the arrival in Eurasia of modern humans from Africa forty-three thousand years ago and the creation of ceremonial burial sites there around twelve thousand years ago. In these graves scientists found the bones of early dogs — no longer wolves — arranged in the protective embrace of human skeletons, purposely buried together. Photographs taken of these fossils as they were originally found leave little question that the deceased humans and dogs shared a deep connection whose exact meaning has been lost to us. Whatever happened between ancient wolves and humans, it gave rise, eventually, to the intimate placement of dogs and people together after death—and to the similarly intimate placement of living family dogs on people's beds all over the world today.

But what *did* occur? And when, exactly, did it happen, and where? What could it reveal about how our own species of ape —descended from a long line of tree dwellers who never buried their dead—somehow adopted this most human of behaviors? And if all domestic dogs are descended from gray wolves, as geneticists have confirmed, and if they share more than 98 percent of their wild ancestors' genetic makeup, then why does the species *Canis lupus familiaris,* when viewed as a whole, look like an unruly group of wildly dissimilar creatures who might have been conjured up by a mad scientist with an overactive imagination?

The answers to these and other questions were written in bones and cells and hidden in plain sight in the familiar behaviors of the dogs at our feet and in our laps. But now, for the first time, scientists have the tools, and the interest, to begin deciphering the clues.

Almost everything that's known about the origins of dogs and humans, and the ways in which we've evolved together, has been learned first through the study of fossils—naturally preserved traces of living organisms that existed in the remote past. Humans have been interested in fossils for as long as there have been humans; both early modern humans and their Neanderthal relatives often used fossilized bones and teeth as jewelry. Later, people prized them as curiosities, but fossils were not always well understood.

The Greek philosopher and scientist Aristotle (384–322 B.C.) believed living things could arise spontaneously from bits of rock or mud that contained "seeds of life," and that fossils were simply incomplete examples or failures of this process. At later times in history, fossils were variously regarded as works of the devil, as creations in rock by a god or gods, as forces of nature in their own right, as the remains of animals and humans lost during the biblical flood of Noah, as dragon bones, and as medicinal cures. What seems obvious today about the natural origins of fossils was regarded as mysterious and even mystical when so little was understood about the physical nature of the world.

But by the seventeenth century, the science of geology had advanced with the realization that the lowest rock layers in any location were deposited there first, and were therefore the oldest; a growing number of naturalists began to recognize fossils as the remains of animals and plants. During the 1700s, fossil collecting became a popular activity among both professional scientists

This diagram illustrates layers of sediment with a fossil embedded in them.

and amateurs, and scientists began to classify and describe fossils and rock strata in a detailed and more consistent way. By the 1830s, geologic features were widely recognized as the product of natural processes—deposition and erosion of mineral layers —acting over long periods of time.

These basic principles of geology, especially the observation that fossil forms changed in a regular and identifiable way over time, greatly influenced the English naturalist Charles Darwin. They provided a basis for his groundbreaking concept of natural selection, which held that naturally occurring variations in plants and animals that provide survival advantages allow those organisms to reproduce in greater numbers than their less "fit" competitors. In this way the characteristics of an individual species change over generations.

Darwin was, in addition to a geologist and naturalist, a lifelong dog lover. For at least twenty years before publishing his groundbreaking 1859 book, *On the Origin of Species,* he had pondered the astonishing variety of canines in his immediate world and found it both puzzling and intriguing. Dogs and scientific curiosity had been his twin passions since childhood, though early in life he'd spent so much time in the countryside with his dogs that his physician father predicted he would never amount to much.

"You care for nothing but shooting, dogs and rat-catching," Darwin later remembered being lectured by his exasperated father, "and you will be a disgrace to yourself and your family."

But Darwin's close observations of the many dogs in his life inspired the revolutionary ideas that would eventually form the basis of his most important work in understanding how species evolve through time. Dogs were his comfort, his constant joy, and his pets, but they were also among his favorite scientific subjects. So many sizes, shapes, colors, and personalities

Charles Darwin (1809–1882)

all grouped together under the single label "dog"! How, he wondered, could all of this variation occur within a single species?

Darwin could only conclude that such dissimilar-looking dogs must have descended from several different wild canine species, including, he surmised, the wolf, jackal, and coyote. But even then, without any plausible explanation for how it could be so, he was taken with the seemingly preposterous idea that such diversity in the dog world *could* have sprung from a single wild ancestor.

"If it could be shown," he wrote, "that the greyhound, bloodhound, terrier, spaniel and bull-dog, which we all know propagate their kind truly, were the offspring of any single species, then such facts would have great weight in making us doubt about the immutability of the many closely allied natural species."

It would mean, Darwin realized, that species could change over time, sometimes in spectacular and surprising ways—a profound idea that conflicted with the then-prevailing belief that species were unchanging parts of a divinely designed hierarchy and that humans were unique, above and unrelated to other animals.

Although highly controversial when first proposed, Darwin's conceptual model, with its large number of examples from nature based on meticulous observations over many years, was gradually accepted by most scientists. By 1890, biologists had rediscovered the long-neglected work of an obscure Austrian monk named Gregor Mendel, who had, more than twenty years earlier, published the results of experiments with garden peas that showed how traits are passed from parent to offspring. With that, scientists finally began to understand the mechanism by which Darwin's natural selection could happen in nature.

By the mid-1900s, advances in the new field of genetics revealed that spontaneous changes in genes —called mutations—can be passed on to offspring. Mutations were provided the source of natural variation that Darwin's theory required, but that he had barely begun to suspect by

Gregor Johann Mendel (1822–1884)

BEFORE DARWIN

Charles Darwin was not the first scientist to speculate that modern dogs might have descended from the gray wolf. General ideas about the evolution of species had been in the air since at least the time of his grandfather, the physician, natural philosopher, and poet Erasmus Darwin, who foreshadowed concepts of evolution and natural selection over time in his *Zoonomia* (1794–96). There Erasmus Darwin wrote, "The strongest and most active animal should propagate the species, which should thence become improved."

In 1809 the French naturalist Jean-Baptiste Lamarck outlined his own belief that the natural environment gives rise to physical changes in animals, in a book called *Zoological Philosophy*. Of wolves and dogs he wrote, "No doubt a single, original race, closely resembling the wolf if indeed it was not actually the wolf, was at some period reduced by man to domestication."

But Lamarck never managed to formulate a mechanism that didn't fly in the face of common sense, let alone the common scientific knowledge of his time. For example, he proposed that the giraffe had gotten its long neck by stretching it to reach leaves high in trees, thus strengthening and gradually lengthening it. He further claimed

An artist's representation of differences between the evolutionary theories of Jean-Baptiste Lamarck and of Charles Darwin.

that such giraffes went on to produce offspring with slightly longer necks, too, passing along, fully formed, a characteristic acquired during an individual's lifetime. Not only did this theory run counter to what anyone who had spent much time around giraffes would have observed directly, but it also contradicted prevailing religious beliefs, which declared that every animal had been divinely created in its perfect, final form at a single time in history.

Shunned by both the religious and scientific communities, Lamarck died in poverty and obscurity in 1829. After Charles Darwin's death fifty-three years later, a hundred more years would pass before advances in science and scientific technology would prove that he'd been correct all along about the essential relationship of dogs and wolves, and so, remarkably, had Lamarck. The truth was found in the genes of living dogs, with their dizzying diversity of appearances and behaviors, and the corresponding genes of the far more similar-looking wolves.

the time he died, some eight years too soon to fully appreciate Mendel's discoveries. By now the complementary sciences of genetics—the study of heredity—and paleontology—the study of fossils—began opening a new window onto a prehistoric world teeming with almost unimaginable forms of life.

Spectacular new fossil discoveries in America and Europe from the mid-1800s onward provided dramatic proof that many prehistoric creatures were very different from those living today, and these variations appeared in consistent changes within the geologic record. Once there had been giant dinosaurs and

A fossilized mammoth skeleton.

A three-dimensional rendering of a *Tyrannosaurus rex* dinosaur skeleton.

flying reptiles; once there had been enormous cats, cave bears, and woolly mammoths; once there had lived dire wolves, five feet long and weighing up to two hundred pounds—the largest canid species known to have ever walked the earth.

Until early in this century, fossil evidence for the beginnings of dog domestication was thought to date from about fourteen thousand years ago; that evidence was unearthed at sites in Switzerland in 1873 and in Oberkassel, Germany, in 1914, when the means to accurately date the bones did not yet exist. At the latter site, the skeleton of a dog was found intentionally buried alongside those of two people. Another burial site, this one twelve thousand years old and found in Israel, contained the skeleton of a puppy buried with that of a woman, her hand resting gently on the puppy's body. Other fossil evidence suggests that the inhabitants of this site were still mainly hunter-gatherers just beginning to establish permanent settlements and on the *verge* of becoming farmers — but already undeniably in a close, intimate association with dogs.

Archaeological evidence of humans and wolves living in such close proximity, in relationships little understood today, has been found at various locations from China to France and England — sites that can date to around forty thousand years old. These wolves were clearly not domesticated, but they were also not the same wolves who shrank from human contact. How, exactly, did they interact with the humans living nearby? When and, more important, *how* those humans were living — as nomadic hunter-gatherers or as people creating permanent settlements based on farming — makes all the difference in understanding that early

ARTIFICIAL SELECTION: NOT THE NATURAL ORDER OF THINGS

Today the World Canine Organization recognizes 340 different dog breeds, while the American Kennel Club acknowledges

This group of dogs shows the extreme variation within the subspecies *Canis lupus familiaris*.

only 167; breed organizations from other countries have their own standards. Dogs are by far the most diverse species on earth—which is even more surprising when we remember that dogs are really the *same* species as gray wolves. Genetically speaking, they're almost identical to wolves, and the two are still so closely related that they can successfully interbreed. If the human species were as diversified as dogs, some adult humans would be thirty-foot-tall giants, and others would be the size of toddlers. In reality, most adult humans are around the same height, between five and six feet.

The reason for this extreme variability in dogs is artificial selection—the intentional manipulation of canine reproduction by humans. But artificial selection can be both intentional and unintentional among dog breeders. That's because genes interact in complex ways that are still not fully understood by geneticists, much less by breeders. Humans may intentionally select for one preferred trait when breeding dogs or any other species, but other, often unforeseen traits will almost invariably piggyback on the trait selected.

Artificial selection operates in the same way as natural selection: naturally occurring mutations (caused by random errors in the replication of DNA sequences as cells divide) that give an animal some kind of survival advantage will, over time, be passed down to successive generations and change the entire species. But natural selection is a slow process, whereas artificial selection can be very fast. That's because humans, rather than Mother Nature, select the traits to be passed along. The environment that shapes genetic changes in nature is replaced by an artificial environment shaped by human preferences.

A large pack of nine wolves gathers on a sunny,
snowy day in Yellowstone National Park.

relationship between the two species *before* some wolves began
to transition toward what would eventually be dogs.

A view long held by many scientists studying dog domestication is that the ancestors of dogs were wolves who began
voluntarily living on the outskirts of early human settlements,
overcoming their fear of humans to sneak food scraps — a much
easier living than hunting down wild horses and reindeer. But
many other biologists and paleontologists remain skeptical of the
idea of self-domesticating, garbage-eating, submissively grovel-
ing wolves on their way to becoming dogs, if for no other reason
than that it seems inconsistent with the known nature of wolves

today—fiercely independent animals still much closer to their ancient roots than today's domesticated dog is. Scientists point to ample evidence that feeding from human garbage dumps produces wolves that are *more* aggressive toward humans, not less so. The dumpster-diving wolf who somehow becomes tame, they reason, simply makes no sense. Others are equally certain the fossil evidence proves just that scenario. Ever-changing evidence and differing interpretations of that evidence have made the science of dog evolution one of the most contentious fields of our time.

HUMANS AND WOLVES:
A COMPLICATED
RELATIONSHIP

Wolves and other wild canids had already been in the world for millions of years before early humans arrived in Eurasia between fifty thousand and forty thousand years ago. They were formidable—an apex predator

Wild wolves display a range of coat colors from light gray to black.

A snarling wolf presents a formidable challenge to any adversary.

well adapted to conditions dramatically different from the African origins of our ancestors. There's no doubt that the human newcomers would have been watching and coexisting with these four-legged rivals for thousands of years before there was ever a dog.

The relationship between humans and wolves, though, has had a dark side from the beginning. Almost as soon as humans and dogs formed a pack, they began persecuting the wild wolves. Once people began keeping livestock, starting with domesticated sheep sometime between eleven thousand and nine thousand years ago, wolves quickly became a problem—and soon a symbol of savagery and greed.

Wolves were legitimately responsible for losses of livestock, but the greater horror was the fear that wolves would kill and devour people. At one time the bite of a wolf, like that of many other wild creatures, could bring death in the form of a terrifying disease—rabies. But of all the potentially rabid animals, only the wolf was considered a demon. In reality, though, wolves were far more likely to run from humans than to approach them, and documented wolf attacks on humans, though not unheard of, have always been quite rare.

During the Middle Ages, an obsession with

Chromolithograph print offered as a prize for children who persuaded ten friends to subscribe to the children's magazine *The Little Corporal,* 1867. Many different versions of this classic fairy tale, "Little Red Riding Hood," have portrayed the Big Bad Wolf as a figure of danger and dread.

THE WOLF TURNED SHEPHERD.

An illustration by Gustave Doré for the classic fable "The Wolf Turned Shepherd," by Jean de la Fontaine, 1870.

wolves launched the first organized effort to obliterate them. A widespread belief in werewolves, the shape-shifting human-wolf creature who could attack, transform, and kill humans at random, led to the near-extermination of northern Europe's wolves, which was essentially complete by the late 1800s.

Europeans who migrated to North America, beginning in the 1600s, brought with them their deep hatred and fear of the wolf. At the time, somewhere between 250,000 and 500,000 wild wolves lived in harmony with many Native Americans tribes and the rest of the ecosystem. Native Americans generally revered the wolf for the very traits that were admirable in people: the wolf lived for the good of the pack, providing food for all, even the old and the sick; he educated his children; and he defended his territory against other wolves.

Like European colonization itself, the war on wolves began in the eastern part of the country, and by the mid-1800s, the last New England wolf was gone.

By the mid-1960s, only a few hundred still survived in the lower forty-eight states. Loss of habitat to urban and suburban development, combined with the destruction of once-abundant bison and other primary prey animals, forced wolves into smaller and smaller ranges. Seeing the wolf as a threat to livestock and wild game populations and public safety, the federal government and most

According to the propaganda accompanying this 1939 photo, titled *U.S. on War Path Against Wolves*: "It may be that dead men tell no tales but the bones of dead wolves are tell-tales of the past and future of these 'bad actors' in preying upon domestic animals in western states. Stanley P. Young, left, is making joint scientific studies with the biological survey and the Smithsonian Institution in analyzing the skulls and other bones of wolves as a character study that may lessen their depredations of livestock in the west. This study may be said to be a new bit of scientific research."

With President Theodore Roosevelt standing directly behind him, Jack Reeves "Catch-'em-alive Jack" Abernathy hoists by the jaw a wild wolf he has just killed with his bare hands on September 12, 1905. Abernathy was a Texas cowboy, appointed in 1910 by an admiring Theodore Roosevelt to be the youngest U.S. marshal in history.

states with wolves instituted bounty programs. Paid wolf hunters unleashed an arsenal of weapons against wild wolves, including guns fired from the ground and the air, fire to destroy their dens, leg-hold traps, gas, and poison.

The last wolf in Yellowstone National Park was killed in 1926, and those in Colorado and Wyoming in 1943. The killing spree continued until, by the mid-1960s, as few as three hundred wild wolves still survived in the extreme northern Midwest. But beginning in the 1930s, researchers started educating officials and the public about large predators' key role in sustaining a balance that allows both animals and vegetation to thrive.

By the late 1950s, state wolf bounty programs were repealed, and legal protections for wolves gradually expanded. In 1973 the Endangered Species Act became law, extending federal protection to wild wolves ranging on federal, state, and private lands. Recovery plans were put into place to save the now-endangered gray wolf of North America.

The wolves began to make a remarkable comeback. In the mid-1990s, an experimental wolf reintroduction was carried out in Yellowstone. Thirty-one wolves from two different regions in Canada were released into the park—a controversial action that has turned out to be a remarkable conservation success. Wolves have recolonized the park and its larger surrounding wilderness area; they are thriving in an ecosystem that had become severely unbalanced with the elimination of its natural, original top predator.

Conservationists and wildlife enthusiasts are thrilled with this outcome, but others—especially game-hunting enthusiasts and ranchers, who now must guard their livestock and even their small pets—are deeply opposed to the return of the wolf, and a number of "protected" wolves have been found shot to death.

For now, wild wolves once more inhabit their ancestral home in North America, and even European wolves have staged a recovery. But opponents of the wolf in America have moved to strip its federal protections, turning wolf management over to individual states. As always, the ultimate fate of the wolf is tied to the shifting values and needs of his fellow predator, humans.

WOLF-DOGS: THOSE SKULLS ARE *HOW* OLD?

The Goyet dog skull.

I n 2008 Mietje Germonpré, a young Belgian paleontologist specializing in Paleolithic carnivores, made a startling discovery. She wondered if dogs might have begun the transition from wolves even earlier than twelve thousand years ago but this had somehow been overlooked in the fossil record. Based at the Royal Belgian Institute of Natural Sciences in Brussels,

Germonpré is not only a scientist but also an animal lover who grew up with, as she recalls, "the kindest dog ever."

Germonpré's own museum housed collections of early canid fossils, including some that had been excavated in the Goyet Cave in Belgium nearly 150 years earlier but had not been examined much since that time. She and her team had already developed and tested a systematic way to distinguish early dogs from wolves that could be applied to fossils. This was the first step to figuring out when ancient wolves had begun to transition to dogs, before tackling the even more daunting questions of where and how this may have happened. It began with precise measurements of the skull anatomy and teeth of some modern wolves, and also of modern dogs representing eleven different breeds.

It came as no surprise that a group of animals as diverse as the domestic dog showed a great variety in the size and shape of individual dogs' skulls. There are more differences between the skulls of a Chihuahua and a collie than there are between those of a weasel and an elephant seal! But like those of other members of the order Carnivora, dog and wolf skulls do share certain distinctive traits, including large brain cases and a well-developed structure called the zygomatic arch, which allows for powerful biting and chewing.

What the scientists hoped to determine was just when the skulls of dogs began to diverge from those of wolves. Did it happen in a single place or many? What would the transformation from wild wolf to domestic dog have looked like when it began? What could the skulls reveal about how humans and dogs began living together in some wholly new way, in a relationship unique in the animal kingdom?

The answers might be found in small changes in the proportion and arrangement of teeth, jawbones, and the width of the skull. Germonpré and her team demonstrated that modern wolves can be accurately distinguished from modern dogs by combining measurements of the proportions of their snouts and the size of their teeth. Almost all modern dogs, they found, have smaller teeth and broader, shorter snouts than do modern wolves. Might not the same be true of *prehistoric* dogs and wolves? If so, analyzing fossils in this specific way, by carefully measuring snouts and teeth and comparing them with the known measurements of modern dogs and wolves, could be a way to separate very early dogs from their wolf cousins. Finding the very earliest dogs, then, could tell scientists when and where wolves first began evolving into dogs.

Based on this approach, scientists found that the institute's collection of ancient canid skulls contained some that were clearly wolves, with long tooth rows and larger teeth, and others that were very early dogs, transitional dogs, or transitional wolves in the process of *becoming* dogs. The early dogs had long tooth rows, like those of wolves, but shorter, broader snouts, more like those of modern dogs. The researchers had expected this, since very early dogs would have still looked much the same as the wild wolves who were their recent ancestors.

The researchers expanded their analysis to include more modern dogs and wolves, young wolves and some captive wolves from zoos. One modern Central Asian shepherd dog was found, based on skull analysis, to resemble the prehistoric dogs, providing a tantalizing suggestion of what such early dogs looked like.

So far, Germonpré and her colleagues had developed and verified an accurate way to recognize prehistoric dogs in the fossil record, based on precise measurements of the fossils themselves. And they had used this technique to identify three previously unclassified prehistoric skulls from their collections as early dogs—one from the Goyet Cave in Belgium and the others from each of two sites in Ukraine. But one key question remained: how old were these skulls?

Germonpré knew that the Belgian cave from which the first of these skulls had been excavated had contained artifacts and animal bones ranging from about 100,000 years ago to about 11,000 years ago. She expected the prehistoric dog skull to be about 12,000 to 14,000 years old, in line with the generally accepted date of dog domestication. But it had never been definitively dated, so that was the necessary next step. A tiny sample from the Goyet skull was sent off to be analyzed by a sophisticated laboratory procedure, invented in the late 1940s, called radiocarbon dating.

The results of this test were astonishing. The Goyet canid had lived some 36,000 years ago! It seemed impossible, but the date was clear and the test conclusive, calculated by a highly reputable lab, with a margin of error of no more than 250 years.

This was more than unexpected. It was stunning.

"When I received the results of the date," Germonpré

recalled, "I was really disappointed. I thought no one would believe it. *I* couldn't believe it."

One reason for her disbelief? If the Goyet skull represented the 36,000-year-old remains of a dog, why had no other early dog fossils been found that might bridge the gap between that date and the next oldest at 14,000 years? Even if it was true, as her team's original hypothesis had stated, that early fossil dogs had been missed because there'd been no good way of recognizing them among the fossils of prehistoric wolves, it seemed unlikely that the Goyet dog would be the *only* one.

Could the explanation lie more in human nature than in dog history? Could it be that until then, no scientists had even asked the question of whether a large canid skull from such an early period could represent a domestic dog? These fossils would have been judged too ancient to be domesticated, since "everyone knew" that dog domestication happened thousands of years later, as humans were transitioning from a hunter-gatherer culture to a more settled lifestyle based on agriculture.

The history of science is filled with flashes of insight made possible by the simple act of keeping an open mind. If you keep looking without preconceptions, hard evidence and careful science will often lead you to the truth. Science will advance another step. Germonpré and her team kept looking.

In 2011 the remains of three more Paleolithic dogs were unearthed at Předmostí, an Upper Paleolithic site in the Czech Republic. The site is littered with the bones of more than a thousand mammoths, as well as tools fashioned of stone and bone,

RADIOCARBON DATING

By the late 1800s, a basic geologic time scale had been worked out. Most geologists recognized that the earth was much older —possibly millions of years older—than previously thought. But there was no widely accepted method to assign a specific age to fossils found buried within the geologic layers. That changed with the discovery of radioactivity in 1896, by the French physicist Henri Becquerel.

Understanding the properties of radioactivity led to the development of a crucial tool for determining the age of ancient artifacts that is based on carbon, an element present in all known life forms. Carbon dating takes advantage of unstable radioactive carbon-14 atoms (so called because their nuclei contain six protons and eight neutrons) produced when cosmic rays from outer space bombard the atmosphere of the earth. The radioactive carbon combines with oxygen atoms to form carbon dioxide, some of which is absorbed by plants and animals as long as they're alive. But once they die, they absorb no additional radioactive carbon, and carbon-14 disappears over time. The ratio of carbon-14 to carbon-12, the most common and abundant natural carbon isotope, can be used to calculate the age of bones and artifacts going back as long as about fifty thousand years.

Sometimes contamination of the artifacts that contain younger organic molecules can distort the dating, making a fossil appear to be thousands of years younger than it is, but improvements in radiocarbon dating techniques have now begun to correct past inaccuracies by removing contaminants. Dates previously thought to be firmly established can, in this way, prove to be older —sometimes requiring a radical rethinking of timelines and the relationships of various ancient species. Currently, radiocarbon dates are calibrated to correct for known fluctuations in the concentration of carbon-14 in the atmosphere over time.

The Předmostí dog skull. A bone, believed to have been placed by humans in the dog's mouth after it died, is clearly visible.

other human artifacts, and the skeletal remains of wild animals, including wolves, foxes, reindeer, horses, bears, wolverines, and hares. One of the ancient dogs was found with a mammoth bone in its mouth. Germonpré and her fellow researchers believe it was inserted there by a human hand after the dog had died.

The bones told the scientists a great deal about these animals and, by extension, about the people whose remains were found near theirs. These were large canids, weighing close to eighty pounds; they would probably have resembled a modern Siberian husky. They were big enough to have been useful for hauling meat, bones, and tusks from mammoth-killing sites to this cave, as well as firewood and other equipment for the

Předmostí people with whom they seem to have lived. With large quantities of mammoth parts available, along with parts of smaller mammals, there would have been plenty of surplus meat to feed the dogs. And there is evidence that when these dogs died, they were buried with reverence and ritual.

Their skulls had been perforated, most likely by humans in order to remove the brains. With so much mammoth meat around, the scientists think it unlikely that these dog brains served as food. What could be the reason for the perforation of skulls, then?

Based on previous studies of fossils from this period, Germonpré believes it may have been for the purpose of some ritual ceremony important to the people of this place and time. Like other northern indigenous people, the Předmostí may have believed that the head contained the spirit or soul. It was common in these cultures to make a hole in the braincase of an animal that had died or been killed so that its spirit might be released.

The mammoth bone in the dog's mouth might signify that it was symbolically "fed" as it was laid to rest with the body of a deceased person, to accompany the soul of the dead human on its journey. Based on her work as an expert in large Ice Age mammals and on what is known of northern Upper Paleolithic cultures, Germonpré believes there may have been many such rituals involving early dogs who associated themselves with Ice Age people.

When Germonpré's team analyzed the three canid skulls, they judged that all three fit easily into the criteria for prehistoric

Mietje Germonpré compares the Goyet dog skull with those of other canids in her office at the Royal Belgian Institute of Natural Sciences in Brussels, Belgium.

dogs: they all had the relatively shorter, wider snouts and smaller teeth than those of wolves. They were dated to almost the same age as the animal now known as the Goyet dog. A separate team of researchers subsequently discovered a thirty-three-thousand-year-old canid skull, showing a similarly shortened snout and other doglike traits, in a cave in the Altai Mountains of Siberia. Evidence for the domestication of dogs in Eurasia during the Upper Paleolithic period seemed to be mounting—a completely unexpected development in the understanding of both human and canine history.

If humans and dogs were living and hunting together as

Sites where ancient dog fossils have been found.

long as thirty-six thousand years ago, much of what scientists thought they knew about the origins of dogs would need to be reconsidered. This would mean that dogs and humans began their long, close association not on the edges of early farming villages, but at a time when nomadic bands of human hunter-gatherers followed herds of woolly mammoths, horses, and reindeer from

The panel of horses found in Chauvet Cave. Many large prey animals are depicted on the walls of Chauvet Cave, but no wolves or dogs are included. Humans — like wolves in that they are at the top of the food chain — may have been assisted in hunting by cooperative early dogs.

place to place in a frozen European landscape. It would suggest a scenario in which nomadic human hunters worked alongside some kind of new wolf—a wolf in the process of becoming a dog—perhaps combining their talents in a cooperative quest to obtain essential protein for both. This could not have been a relationship marked by dominance and submission, but rather a voluntary association of equals, with humans providing extra food and protection to cooperative wolves, and in turn relying on the acute senses of these canids to help track prey and to protect them from other carnivorous mammals.

Some scientists believe it isn't a question of either-or, wolf or dog. Animals such as the Goyet dog, although different from modern dogs in certain features of their skull anatomy, were nevertheless also different from modern and ancient wolves and might best be considered "transitional" dogs, probably descended from evolutionary lines that went extinct rather than leaving a genetic trail that could be directly traced to today's dogs.

How might domestication have begun as long as thirty-six thousand years ago? Long before human settlements were formed, small bands of hunters lived by tracking and killing large mammals; meat was their primary food. Hunting would have resulted in leftover carcasses that wolves, wolf-dogs, and many other carnivorous scavengers would have found very useful. Humans, like wolves, were capable of taking prey much larger than themselves. Mammoths and horses killed during a hunt were probably not consumed down to the marrowbones before human hunters moved on.

Wolves lurked in the shadows of human camps, waiting, and helped themselves to the carcasses when the humans were gone. Another possible scenario: humans followed wolf packs tracking prey, with the objective of moving in at the last moment to make the kill and take the meat for themselves if they could.

Certain, though not all, wolves and humans would have become well acquainted as the distance between them shrank over time, long before one particularly bold or curious wolf became the first protodog. This preadaptation of some wild wolves to human contact may have been underway long before humans began living in settlements and creating the first garbage dumps;

wolves living in such close proximity would have begun diverging from their more wild counterparts in fundamental ways, long before the differences became visible in the shapes of their skulls and arrangement of their teeth.

Why does any of this matter? Are the contradictory theories just quibbles among scientists eager to stake a claim in an increasingly crowded, fast-changing, and attention-grabbing area of research? Or is the story of when, where, and especially *how* wolves became dogs about something deeper than simply settling on a date for when the two species split? What circumstances could have led to that split? What was it about the relationship of Paleolithic humans and wolves that eventually brought them together in a whole new way, setting both canine and primate on a profoundly changed evolutionary path? Was it human agriculture and ingenuity that set the stage for the unprecedented partnership between human and wolf, as less fearful wolves simply exploited the trash heaps they found on the outskirts of human settlements?

Or was it, instead, something much deeper and more interesting that brought human and wolf together? Did some wild wolves overcome their basic instincts—aggression and fear—to reap the advantages of a closer association with humans? Or was the affinity formed still earlier, built upon something inherent in the basic nature of both?

The Altai dog may have something to tell us about this. Discovered in a cave in the northwestern part of Siberia's Altai Mountains in 1975, the complete skull and mandible of a dog-like canid dating from thirty-three thousand years ago were an incredible find. Was this dog just another relic of a failed early attempt at domestication, as many believed the Goyet dog to be?

The Siberian cave also contained the frozen mummified remains of mammals and birds, including more than seventy-thousand bones and bone fragments from large mammals, including foxes, cave hyenas, gray wolves, and brown bears. There were also the remains of numerous hares and ibex goats. Scientists think the cave was used as a den, primarily by hyenas but also, at various times in antiquity, by bears and wolves, who may have fed on the smaller animals found in the cave. Disappointingly, no human artifacts have been recovered from this cave, but the presence of small pieces of charcoal and charred bones suggests strongly that ancient people occasionally visited the Altai cave, too.

Was the Altai canid a very early dog or just an unusual wolf? It would be almost forty years before this question was finally answered: The answer was a direct result of new scientific knowledge—a new way to analyze very old bones that didn't rely solely on human interpretation of fossil forms.

THE SCIENTIFIC METHOD AND THE VALUE OF WHAT-IF

Fossils are tangible evidence of the past, but deciphering what's written in those bones is part hard science and part speculation. Both are essential components of science. The first is based on solid evidence and meant to be judged by scientific peers and others accordingly; the second is less intended to support any predetermined conclusion than it is to encourage thought and additional research. Speculative research can, and often does, lead to new discoveries and understanding that enlarge the body of human scientific knowledge, but only if the author is scrupulous about distinguishing what is known for sure, what is probable, and what might be possible *and* can be tested to see if it's true. It's the difference, in the words of the *New York Times* science reporter James Gorman, between "what is" and "what if."

Since at least the seventeenth century, scientists the world over have followed a set of techniques and standards for investigating the natural world; this is known as the scientific method. By this method, observations about the world and events that happen in it can be investigated, new knowledge can be acquired, and previous knowledge can be corrected and integrated into what is learned today. But to be considered scientifically valid, research must be based on observable, measurable evidence that follows the principles of logic. The basic stages or steps that all scientists strive to follow include systematic observation, measurement, experimentation, and the formulation, testing, and modification of hypotheses.

A hypothesis is a proposed explanation for an observed phenomenon. Often scientists base hypotheses on previous observations that can't be satisfactorily explained with the available scientific theories. Proposing a hypothesis can be a very creative process, as scientists open their minds to possibilities and "what if" questions. Some of the most important discoveries in the scientific world have been arrived at by those willing to ask such open-ended questions. But to be a *scientific* hypothesis, the proposed explanation must be testable, and it must undergo extensive and rigorous testing before it may be accepted as a scientific theory. Previously accepted scientific theories have, at times, been proven false in the light of new information. In the scientific meaning of the word, then, a theory has been tested and generally accepted as an accurate explanation of the observation or phenomenon being explored. A working hypothesis is a provisionally accepted theory, pending further research.

The way scientists work is to observe reality, and then to let reality speak for itself, supporting a hypothesis when its predictions are confirmed, and challenging it if its predictions prove false. So in science, asking (or formulating) the right question is as important as finding the right answers, since both are necessary to discover the truth. After proposing a hypothesis, researchers must design experimental studies to test the hypothesis by finding out whether the predictions that follow from it are true.

The reason for such strict standards is to keep scientific inquiry as objective as possible. Scientists are also expected to document, archive, and share (often in the form of peer-reviewed, published papers) all of the data collected and the methods used, so that other scientists can attempt to reproduce and verify the results. Without these steps, science isn't really *science;* it's more a kind of storytelling. Imagination and belief are one kind of truth, but science is a different level of truth. For thousands of years people have recognized that knowledge requires both.

A MEETING OF MINDS

Though humans and chimpanzees share nearly 99 percent of our
DNA, we are very different species in both appearance and behavior.
It seems apparent that humans would be able to live in the company
of dogs much more easily than in the company of chimps.

W hen it comes to our relationship with dogs, dog
evolution is only half of the story. The other half
is a bit more personal to us: *human* evolution.
When Charles Darwin published his transformative theory of
evolution through natural selection in 1859, he included almost

nothing specifically about *human* evolution. It wasn't that he doubted human beings were subject to the same mechanism of natural selection as other species, but expressing this view was risky at the time. He knew it would rock the foundations of religious orthodoxy and likely meet with great public resistance. It was a full twelve years later—years during which Darwin conducted meticulous studies of orchids, barnacles, pigeons, and

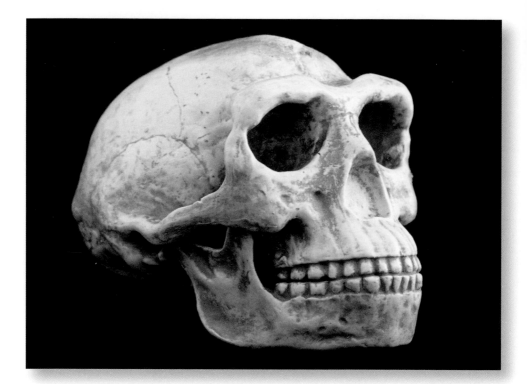

A *Homo erectus* fossil skull. *Homo erectus* (meaning "upright man") is an extinct species of hominid that lived throughout most of the Pleistocene geological epoch. Its earliest fossil evidence dates to 1.9 million years ago and the most recent to 70,000 years ago. It is generally thought that *H. erectus* originated in Africa and spread from there, migrating throughout Eurasia as far as Soviet Georgia, India, Sri Lanka, China, and Indonesia. Some scientists argue that the species arose first, or separately, in Asia.

other "lower" life forms—that he finally published his thoughts on human evolution in *The Descent of Man*.

He began by building a detailed comparative analysis of various anatomical features of the modern human form and of other mammals. He compared similar embryonic features and body structures, and pointed out the existence in humans of "rudimentary organs"—what scientists now call vestigial structures —such as the coccyx (tailbone) and muscles of the ear, which, in humans, have apparently lost much of their original purpose. Such "organs," Darwin reasoned, could be explained only as body parts that had been useful in one of humankind's preexisting forms.

The term "coevolution" was not a part of Darwin's argument about human descent, but his recognition of vestigial structures leads directly to it. And it seems likely that he would be delighted to know that today most evolutionary biologists believe dogs probably had everything to do with the fact that some 85 percent of humans cannot wiggle our ears, though virtually every dog can effortlessly accomplish this feat. Scientists believe that when early modern humans began their close association with wolves (or wolf-dogs), they no longer needed such an acute sense of hearing. That crucial function was delegated, in some part, to the dogs.

USE IT OR LOSE IT?

Why do we have vestigial organs if they're no longer useful to us? Because almost everything about our lives, from the foods we eat to the dangers we face in our world, and therefore our physical bodies, has changed since our ancestors first climbed down from the trees and began walking on two feet. Take goose bumps, for example. That's what we call the tiny elevations in the skin that we sometimes feel when we're cold, frightened, or experiencing other intense emotional states; the hair on the back of our necks, arms, and legs suddenly stands on end. Though called goose bumps because of a certain resemblance to the skin of a plucked fowl, this phenomenon is more closely related to our furrier fellow mammals. Everyone has seen the "hackles" of a dog standing straight up when the animal feels especially excited or threatened, or when it's shivering in the cold. This is caused by

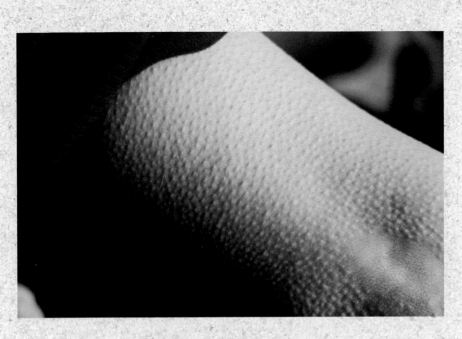

Goose bumps are an example of vestigial reminders of our evolutionary past that connect us to other mammals, including wolves and dogs.

tiny, involuntary muscle contractions at the base of hair follicles. In hair-covered animals, this response can serve two purposes: it will instantly make an animal appear bigger and more threatening to a potential attacker, and it can provide extra insulation to help warm the body. Though humans are now almost hairless on most of our bodies, we owe goose bumps to our more hirsute primate ancestors.

Long before the term "coevolution" was conceived, Darwin believed in the power of dogs to help shape human evolution. A related idea—evolution by sexual selection—was an important corollary to Darwin's theory of evolution by natural selection. In Darwin's view of human evolution, people who had the most dogs would have reproduced more successfully than those who had none. Therefore humans associating with dogs became more "fit" than their dogless counterparts, and that meant that more of their physical traits were passed down to succeeding generations, becoming more widespread in the population of human beings.

Darwin's theory of natural selection was all-encompassing; he recognized that the selection of particular traits in the human population over time was not limited to physical characteristics. From anatomical similarities among humans and other mammals, Darwin moved on to argue a similarity of *mental* processes. This, he asserted, was clear evidence that humans' mental characteristics are inherited in the same manner as physical traits, and they exist on a continuum among different species. In a living world governed by evolutionary processes, there could be no real distinction between the mind and the body, or between human and animal.

Charles Darwin correctly identified the evolutionary roots of humans in the great apes, such as this mother orangutan and her baby.

Like other naturalists of his time, Darwin believed that animals differed from humans largely in degree, not in kind. As one moved from lower to higher orders of animals, the influence of simple instinct over behavior declined and that of intelligence increased—with dogs and horses close to the top of Darwin's

THE DOG FANCY

For most of their long history, dogs had been the masters of their own breeding, with only limited interference from humankind. Sexual selection, a cornerstone of Darwin's theory of evolution, produced a stable and relatively uniform dog with several basic variations. These variations created functional types that humans found useful: hunting dogs, guard dogs, war dogs, herding dogs, and a few small pet dogs, the toy breeds. Then, seemingly overnight, human manipulation of canine form and function intensified into a near frenzy, finally culminating in the obsessive "dog fancy" of Victorian Great Britain in the late 1800s.

Tension between the wealthy, mostly rural upper classes of British society and a growing urban middle class fed the frenzy to breed new dogs, and to meticulously record and guard the breeding practices that produced these supposedly aristocratic dogs. These dogs had "pure" bloodlines reflecting the innate superiority (in the case the upper class) or the respectability and worthiness (for the rising middle class) of their breeders and owners. Carefully bred dogs suddenly became a vehicle for human class identification and striving.

As fox hunting became ever more fashionable, it required appropriate dress and accessories. So it was that foxhounds became the first dogs intensively designed for their fashionable looks as well as their enhanced function. Hound packs were bred to be uniform in color (usually white with brown

A hunt master with his pack of pedigreed hounds at the start of the annual Boxing Day Hunt in Cirencester, England.

The red fox, singled out as a target by many traditional hunts in Great Britain, the United States, and many other countries, is just one of many wild canids in the world. Some hunts in the western and southwestern United States pursue the coyote instead of the red fox.

patches) and in coat quality (smooth and dense, not shaggy or wiry). They also needed stamina, keen noses, quick intelligence to outwit the fox, full-throated voices, and tractable personalities.

This genteel system would change radically when the concept of canine pedigrees filtered down to urban middle-class hunters by the middle of the nineteenth century. The filtering down was helped along by Queen Victoria herself, a popular monarch who reigned from 1837 until her death in 1901 and who was a great dog lover. The queen kept a canine menagerie that included well-bred dogs of all sizes and shapes, from greyhounds to tiny Pomeranians. It amounted to a royal endorsement of the dog fancy.

Dog fanciers of more modest means adored their dog-loving queen, but they also looked with envy on the lifestyles of the rural elite and longed to emulate them. What better place to start than with breeding and showing dogs? Dogs didn't require huge outlays of money or country estates to keep them, unlike horses and the other pedigreed livestock kept by the landed gentry.

These new dog enthusiasts were often more concerned with the appearance of their dogs than with their function, probably because appearance

Great Britain's Queen Victoria (1819–1901) was more often photographed with one or another of her favorite dogs. She was a great dog lover all her life, and an inspiration to those caught up in the "dog fancy" movement of Victorian Britain.

A young Victorian girl with her lapdog, dressed in jinglebells and lace.

was easier to manipulate through breeding and could instantly proclaim to the world the "excellence" of their dogs. This, in turn, reflected the value of the owner and breeder. Soon enough, such excellence began to command high prices for stud dogs, stud fees, and puppies.

The first formal dog show held in England took place in Newcastle on June 28, 1859. The event was strictly aimed at gentleman sport hunters and their gun dogs. There were only two classes —pointers and setters. Sixty entries filled those two classes. The show was such a success that a larger display of sporting dogs took place a few months later in Birmingham. The following year, this show added thirteen classes for "non-sporting" dogs—namely pets. This addition was greeted with overwhelming public enthusiasm, and by 1890 major dog shows in London attracted up to two thousand entries each, with slightly more modest shows cropping up in smaller towns and cities.

Something had to be done to preserve the integrity of the whole enterprise. So an official kennel club was founded in 1873, which aimed to combat breeder fraud by establishing the pedigrees of all exhibited dogs. The unspoken goal was to limit competition to a screened and approved segment of the canine population, thus keeping out the human "undesirables."

Fanciers created detailed breed standards, almost entirely based on appearance, with arbitrary rules about acceptable colors as well as other physical traits of these new breeds. The functional or behavioral standards that were included seemed vague and whimsical, almost tacked on as an afterthought, and much more difficult to demonstrate than the acceptable external traits such as coat color, height, shape of head and ears, and the set of a tail.

Once the standards were in place, breeders

and fanciers rushed to create dogs that adhered to them, and even exceeded them. Extreme breed traits, like the "right" length of muzzle or size of head, came to equal a superior dog in the minds of fanciers and dog show judges alike. The elevation of "purely bred" dogs meant that those who were not so pure were looked down upon, as were their "lower-class" owners. With few exceptions, the less a dog resembled its wild wolf forebears, the more improved and noble the dog was considered to be.

In 1873 the British Kennel Club was established to enforce rules and ethical standards, in effect protecting certain established breeders and creating a monopoly in the purebred dog trade. In 1884 the American Kennel Club was established with the same purpose. Breed standards were maintained through intensive inbreeding and scrupulous pedigree records.

Breeders started producing dogs so varied that they seemed as different from each other, and from their common ancestor, as if they were separate species altogether. Like Frankenstein's monster, these new, improved dogs were hailed as a triumph of science as well as a symbol of status.

hierarchy, right below humans and apes. Focusing his general argument primarily on apes (our closest human relatives) and dogs, he identified similar mental abilities and characteristics demonstrated by these animals and shared with human beings, such as love, cleverness, kindness, and altruism.

Darwin's big idea in *The Descent of Man* was that human evolution operated in much the same way as that of other organisms: as a gradual process with no defined starting (or, for that matter, ending) point, by which *Homo sapiens* had changed over time. Just as with any organism, random individual mutations that provided survival advantages were passed along to succeeding generations of humans. And just as he had earlier written that dogs must share an extinct common ancestor with their closest living relatives, wolves (and, he thought, other wild canids), so humans must share an extinct common ancestor with *their* closest living relatives, the great apes. He wrote, "In a series of forms graduating insensibly from some ape-like creature to man as he now exists, it would be impossible to fix on any definite point when the term 'man' ought to be used. But this is a matter of very little importance . . . man still bears in his bodily frame the indelible stamp of his lowly origin."

Remarkably, given the limited knowledge of his time, Darwin correctly hypothesized that the extinct common ancestor of

A large male silverback. Gorillas are another close relative of *Homo sapiens*.

all humans must have originated in Africa, home to gorillas and chimpanzees. He was hampered in making the same intuitive leap about the origin of dogs only by his uncertainty of whether dogs were descended from several wild canids or only one.

Now we know it was only one: the gray wolf. But there were no wolves in Africa when early modern humans first emerged there. Somehow, somewhere, the descendants of African apes and Eurasian wolves crossed paths and began interacting in a way that no such distantly related species had ever done before or since.

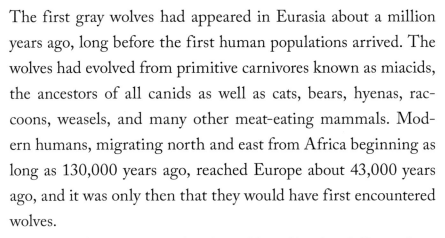

The first gray wolves had appeared in Eurasia about a million years ago, long before the first human populations arrived. The wolves had evolved from primitive carnivores known as miacids, the ancestors of all canids as well as cats, bears, hyenas, raccoons, weasels, and many other meat-eating mammals. Modern humans, migrating north and east from Africa beginning as long as 130,000 years ago, reached Europe about 43,000 years ago, and it was only then that they would have first encountered wolves.

Soon after their arrival in this cold, arid land so different from their ancestral home, European early modern humans, popularly known as Cro-Magnons (named after the area in southwestern France where their remains were first discovered), quickly established themselves as a dominant predator. The landscape was alive with other large carnivores, including wolves, several species of wild cats, hyenas, and at least one other hominid group that had arrived almost 200,000 years before them. All had to compete in hunting the large plant-eaters that provided much of the protein that sustained them; each species had developed specific strategies for improving their odds of success in capturing and killing prey. Hyenas, for example, most often hunted alone or in groups of two or three, but wolves almost always hunted cooperatively, in larger packs. So did humans, though it's not known for certain when they first adopted this practice.

"Social" predators such as wolves and humans were generally social only with their own kind, avoiding or aggressively driving away any outsiders perceived as potential threats. Co-operation with a competing predatory species for their mutual survival was certainly not natural behavior for a predator at the top of the food chain. The question of who had the idea first—human or wolf—has yet to be settled for sure. But no one doubts that this unlikely alliance became a unique bond that profoundly changed both species, and the world.

Even though they evolved in distant parts of the world, from seemingly dissimilar species and in entirely different climates and circumstances, early human beings and wolves were more alike than different in important ways. Both were big-brained, highly social, and supremely successful hunters who lived in small family groups, caring for and protecting their young. Perhaps the alliance required only that they meet somewhere along the trail for the process of coevolution to be sparked. When early humans migrated out of Africa, first traveling to the Arabian Peninsula, Australia, and the western Pacific region before expanding their range to Asia and Europe, the stage was set for an eventual fateful encounter.

But another species of early human was already inhabiting

More than most primates, gray wolves are very social. These three are playing together.

these same lands, having descended from a shared ancestor who had left Africa thousands of years earlier. Evidence for this other species of hominids was already known to the world in Darwin's time. Just three years before he published his theory of evolution in 1859, workers had discovered a skull and partial skeleton buried deep in a German lime quarry in the Neander Valley, near Düsseldorf; they guessed the bones might be the remains of an ancient cave bear. The mine's owner turned the material over to a local teacher and amateur naturalist, who then brought it to an anatomist at the University of Bonn. Together, the two men identified the bones as *human*, not bear—but they were distinctly different from the bones of any modern humans. A few months later, the anatomy professor announced publicly that the fossilized remains of an ancient, extinct human species had been found.

This electrifying claim was still in the air when Darwin's *On the Origin of Species* appeared in England. Both events inspired a passionate search for our evolutionary origins that continues to this day. The new field of paleoanthropology was born.

Neanderthal Man, or *Homo neanderthalensis,* was a species closely related to our own, *Homo sapiens,* whose branch of the family tree had left Africa long before our ancestors did. They lived in Eurasia from about 200,000 to 30,000 years ago, during the last Ice Age, and they are our closest known extinct relatives. Since that first discovery, the bones of some four hundred Neanderthal individuals have been found over a wide area. The more we learn about them, the more we understand how similar they were to us.

Despite the common (and now discredited) stereotype of Neanderthals as unintelligent, brutish cavemen, they seem to have been comparable with modern humans in many ways. They fashioned advanced tools, had a language that may have included spoken words, and lived in small but complex social groups. Judging from at least one archaeological site in eastern Ukraine, some Neanderthals may have built dwellings using animal bones, and there's evidence they may also have fashioned dugout boats; they may have sailed those boats on the Mediterranean Sea more than 100,000 years ago. Though they were once thought to have been almost entirely carnivorous, new analyses of 50,000-year-old fecal remains from a site once occupied by Neanderthals in southern Spain revealed they also ate cooked vegetables on occasion. This shows that they knew how to make fire. They also buried their dead, and they carved ornamental objects out of animal bones. Revised dating of cave paintings from Spain's northern coast has also led some archaeologists to conclude that Neanderthals may have been responsible for some of the cave paintings long attributed to modern humans.

At the same time, the now-extensive international collection of Neanderthal fossil remains shows that the average Neanderthals' appearance would have been noticeably different from ours. They were physically stronger, heavier, and stockier than modern humans, though they were about the same height. Their facial features were different, too, with a receding chin and forehead and a somewhat protruding nose.

And they had large brains—larger than ours—though the relative size of different parts of their brains also differed from ours. All of this can be read in the shape of their bones, but in recent years, genetic analysis of those bones has given us even more details that suggest tantalizing portraits of individual

Neanderthals—as varied in appearance as their human cousins. Despite their usual depiction as dark, hairy people, for example, at least some Neanderthals are thought to have had red or blond hair, along with a light skin tone.

From the time anatomically modern humans, *Homo sapiens,* arrived in Europe and Asia about forty-four thousand years ago, they coexisted with Neanderthals, perhaps for as long as five thousand years. Though evidence suggests that they may have occasionally interacted and even interbred, for the most part the two big-brained hominids would have been rivals, competing for the same sources of food in a harsh landscape. Neanderthals had been thriving in Europe for thousands of years, during most of which time our own ancestors hadn't yet migrated out of Africa. They had been a top predator, adapting successfully to a dramatically changing climate many times, but within just a few thousand years after modern humans arrived on the scene, they were gone.

Why?

This is one of the most perplexing questions, one that has intrigued evolutionary biologists for generations. Now some scientists think they may have uncovered at least part of the answer.

Neanderthal extinction has long been attributed to the arrival of modern humans in Europe just a few thousand years earlier. Many other large mammals also went extinct during the period following the arrival of modern humans, including some leading predators — the cave lion, cave bear, cave hyena, and scimitar cat, among others — as well as noncarnivorous species such as the woolly mammoth, woolly rhinoceros, and many others. Though hunting by humans has been the leading theory to explain why so many animals vanished from Europe in the late Pleistocene, climate change was also a factor in the profound transformation of the world. Natural global warming caused vast ice sheets to shift northward, giving way to more closed-in woodlands and forests. Hunting practices that had succeeded in colder periods no longer worked, and populations of hunters moved in search of more hospitable conditions. Instead of relying primarily on large herd mammals for food as the land warmed, hominid hunters began shifting to hunting birds and smaller game, and to foraging wild plants for survival.

By this time, Neanderthal populations were already shrinking and becoming more fragmented and less genetically diverse; they would have been more vulnerable to both changing climate and invasion by modern humans. But they had already survived major climate shifts over thousands of years, and the idea that

Neanderthals were simply overrun and exterminated by modern humans with vastly superior intelligence is not what the fossil record and genetic analysis show. In fact, most scientists today believe Neanderthals were an equally "advanced" culture, but one greatly disadvantaged by poverty and hardship and by the isolation of living in small, scattered groups with no means of communicating with one another. It's likely that climate change and pressure from modern humans both played a part in the Neanderthals' demise.

If we factor in new evidence of genetic exchange (through interbreeding) between some modern humans and Neanderthals, we get another scenario, which is increasingly favored by some scientists: Neanderthals were largely *assimilated* into modern human culture over several thousand years, through interbreeding and cultural exchange, rather than simply succumbing to modern human aggression. But none of these explanations alone seems to fully answer the question of what happened to the Neanderthals, and how modern humans emerged as the dominant and only hominid left standing. Scientists across disciplines continue to search for answers to this intriguing and fundamental question of human history.

Pat Shipman is an American paleoanthropologist who has studied and written about Neanderthal culture extensively. She's a storyteller as well as a scientist, and is not afraid to ask big what-if questions, even as she designs rigorous methods to test their validity. Here's one such question: what if dogs, as a uniquely human invention, were the unacknowledged key to human survival in Paleolithic Eurasia—a kind of secret weapon that allowed modern humans to prevail over their Neanderthal cousins? This is a big idea that, for now, remains in the realm of speculation. But as a hypothesis firmly grounded in solid science, it's much more than idle speculation.

Shipman, a respected author of many books about early humans, fossils, and the lives of scientists, as well as numerous papers for both scientific journals and the popular press, is one of many scientists convinced by the weight of evidence that dogs were domesticated much earlier than previously assumed, as demonstrated by the Goyet, Předmostí, and Altai fossils. Building on this insight, she suggests that such a radically revised timeline of dog domestication may help explain the mysterious disappearance of the Neanderthal people less than 10,000 years after modern humans invaded the area Neanderthals had successfully inhabited for 250,000 years.

Dogs are at the heart of an even bigger idea that Shipman calls "the animal connection." Living in close, intimate contact with animals, she says, is an integral part—perhaps the *most important* part—of a uniquely human nature that emerged soon after humans began eating meat and hunting animals to obtain what became their essential source of protein and energy.

Humans became predators, and that changed everything.

This is what we know: Modern humans and Neanderthals inhabited Europe simultaneously for several thousand years, beginning a little less than forty-five thousand years ago. During that time, humans increased in number and prospered, while Neanderthal populations contracted and eventually died out completely. Humans are still there—and everywhere on the planet—researching and inventing, cracking the genetic code of life, engineering worldwide communications networks, and exploring the far reaches of outer space, while Neanderthals have left little behind except the silent bones of their dead and traces of their genes in some of the humans who survived them.

What gave modern humans such a decisive edge? In considering this vexing question, paleoanthropologists trace our species all the way back to our evolutionary transformation from tree-dwelling African primate to far-ranging, swift-moving biped leaving home for distant and unfamiliar lands, and along the way acquiring a whole new diet and way of life.

To become successful carnivores, early humans needed to develop certain essential skills. They had to invent tools to kill, skin, and cut the meat of animals; they needed language or other means of symbolic communication to cooperate in the hunt and to pass down these necessary skills to others in their clan; and they needed, eventually, to domesticate other species of animals, partly to gain a more reliable source of protein.

The first skill—toolmaking—was learned more than 2.6 million years ago, with the invention of simple stone tools by early humans in Africa. By the time groups of humans had left

Africa and arrived in Eurasia, their toolkits had become much more sophisticated and diverse, incorporating other materials—bone, antler, and ivory—in addition to stone.

It's harder to know just when humans developed language, since spoken words leave no trace in the fossil record. But scientists can tell from hominid fossils that both early humans and Neanderthals were anatomically capable of producing some type of speech, though we have no way of knowing what they may

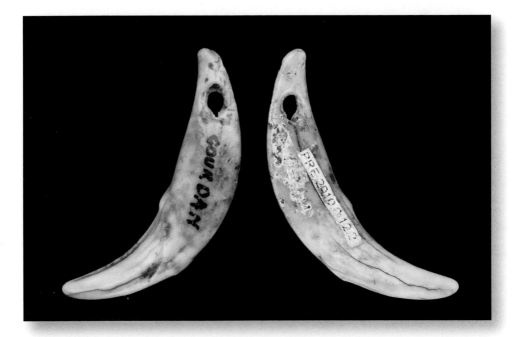

A drilled canine tooth of *Canis lupus*, the gray wolf, that was likely worn as part of a necklace by a Paleolithic human during the Magdalenian period, sometime between 17,000 and 12,000 years ago. It was found in Gourdan Cave in Haute-Garonne, France, also known as Elephant Cave. The wearing of wolf teeth as ornaments by ancient people of that region supports the idea that this was an animal of great symbolic importance.

have talked about or the sound of that speech. It could have been short, muttered sentences; it could have been singing.

But if we think about what language is, we notice that it comes down to communication and to symbolic, abstract thinking. Language is what allowed humans to share important knowledge with other humans; it allowed people to "function as if they had certain types of knowledge without having to acquire them individually," as Shipman explains.

Spoken and written language, with symbols universally understood by one's tribe or clan, is one type of communication; another one is art—symbolic representations of vital information recorded for others to see and understand. Whether painted on rock walls or carved in bone, the art of early humans is filled with information about the animals in their world.

To successfully hunt animals—many of whom were very large, very ferocious, or both—Paleolithic people needed to pay keen attention to the movements and behaviors of other creatures. Detailed, comprehensive knowledge of the animals who shared their world could mean the difference between eating and starving, and between finding dinner and *becoming* dinner for another predator. Sharing that knowledge with others was imperative, since cooperative hunting was the only way to succeed. So it's no surprise that animals are so eloquently and accurately portrayed in prehistoric cave art and artifacts left behind by our distant ancestors. Though no one knows for certain what the purpose of cave drawings and carvings may have been, at

This is a replica of a 26,000-year-old ivory carving of a mammoth found at Předmostí, Czech Republic. It's another example of the flowering of art and culture among humans of that time, which some scientists believe was aided by their association with early dogs and the survival advantages that the partnership offered to both species.

the very least they represent an illustrated field guide to ancient predators and prey.

What's surprising is that while animals are by far the most popular subject of Paleolithic art, humans and canids are only rarely depicted. It's unclear why, but one theory is that creating the likeness of a human may have been, for reasons unknown to us today, considered taboo. Another possibility is that if the point of such drawings was to describe animals hunted for food, these likenesses were simply unnecessary. Though humans and wolves often lived in close proximity, it appears from the assemblages of bones uncovered at ancient hunting sites that neither routinely considered the other as potential or ideal prey.

At the time the Goyet dog lived in Belgium some thirty-six thousand years ago, gray wolves inhabited all of the Northern Hemisphere; they were the most widespread mammal on the earth. They were also a top predator, a distinction they shared with human hunter-gatherers. It's easy to imagine that humans would have noticed and admired the advanced hunting skills of wolves—their ability to anticipate where their prey would move, to track them using their highly developed senses of smell, hearing, and sight, and to follow them tirelessly, working in teams to make the all-important kill.

But it's hard to imagine how early humans could have conceived of the idea of domesticating wolves; nothing like it had ever been done before. Was it a chance event that started it, or a revolutionary idea in the minds of some ancient humans?

And what of the wolves? Did observing humans at close range cause wolves to become more cooperative, or might it have been—just as likely—the other way around?

Friederike Range and Zsófia Virányi of the Wolf Science Center in Ernstbrunn, Austria, have suggested that wolves, long before domestication, already possessed the very sociability and cooperativeness that made a partnership with humans almost inevitable. They've called this the Canine Cooperation Hypothesis. This means that wolves, to become dogs, didn't need to change their basic nature and become more attentive

Gray wolves bond for life, and bonded pairs are the center of the social structure of the pack.

toward and tolerant of humans, because being highly social and cooperative within their packs *was* their basic nature, just as it was for humans. Some scientists even suggest it was wolves who were the *more* social, cooperative species, wolves who taught the big-brained, more competitive primates—humans—how to cooperate with other members of their own family pack instead of fighting with them for dominance.

Coevolution, again, occurs when random mutations in two species sharing an environment provide a survival advantage to both. But in the case of wolves and humans, it's worth asking what survival advantages could have drawn two rival predators together in the first place. Besides behavioral traits that wolves and humans already had in common, each species had special attributes that they brought to the partnership. Humans had sharp tools, hands to grasp those tools, and the ability to strategize; wolves had sharp teeth and highly developed senses of smell and hearing.

On the other hand, wolves didn't *need* to scavenge the leftovers of humans to survive because they were already supremely successful hunters, as were Paleolithic humans. Why take such a huge risk? Part of the answer to this puzzle may be that wolves, like humans, have individual personalities, strengths, and weaknesses that vary from one animal to another. Perhaps the partnership was between humans struggling to outcompete their Neanderthal cousins and a less aggressive population of wolves who found it advantageous to help the nearly hairless, two-legged predator locate, track, and surround the prey, but to leave the actual killing to the well-armed humans. In this cooperative way, the stage could have been set for coevolution. Over time, some traits in both wolves and humans would have changed in tandem, becoming stronger in one species and weaker in the other. Instead of competing, the two would now begin to cooperate in a new partnership—to delegate tasks and specialize in certain aspects of the hunt.

For a few thousand years after humans arrived in Eurasia, Neanderthals hung on, inhabiting a vast area from present-day England east to Uzbekistan and south nearly to the Red Sea. They had survived repeated periods of advancing and retreating glaciers, which caused drastic interruptions in their food chain. When glaciers moved in and edible plants became scarcer, Neanderthals adapted, relying more on hunting large, hoofed animals such as the reindeer and wild horses that grazed the steppes and tundras.

The invaders—*Homo sapiens*—would have hunted the same animals, directly competing with Neanderthals as well as with other carnivores. But these newcomers almost immediately did something entirely new: they started killing large numbers of mammoths, the massive plant-eating mammals that had only been occasional prey for Neanderthals.

Dozens of archaeological sites scattered across central and eastern Europe, dating from forty thousand to about fifteen thousand years ago, contain the remains of as many as a hundred or more mammoths each; some of the sites also contain huts constructed of mammoth bones and tusks. These strange collections of fossils have perplexed researchers for years. So many dead mammoths in a single place, with few of their bones showing signs of gnawing by other animals or cuts by human tools.

Scientists believe most of these mammoths did not die of natural causes. Large herds of them—animals that stood nine to eleven feet tall at the shoulder and weighed about six tons—must have been killed in one place, butchered, and somehow moved to these central camps for storage. None of the multiple mammoth-laden sites found so far dates from before modern humans arrived in Europe, when Neanderthals were the only hominids around, and none of the sites has been found to contain Neanderthal remains or artifacts. Whatever else they may mean, these masses of mammoth bones provide strong evidence that Neanderthals killed mammoths on a much smaller and more infrequent scale than modern humans did.

One of the largest "mammoth megasites," as Shipman calls them, is at Předmostí, the twenty-six-thousand-year-old remnant of early human habitation where early wolflike protodogs, like the one with a mammoth bone placed in its jaws after death, were identified. The remains from at least 105 mammoths were found at this location alone.

How were early modern humans able to accomplish such spectacularly successful mammoth hunting when Neanderthals, evidently, were not? Neanderthal artifacts show that they had effective hunting tools; fossil remains suggest they were apparently as intelligent as the human invaders, and much stronger and more robust. After thousands of years, they should have been better adapted to their environment than the humans, only newly out of Africa. But somehow they were soon outcompeted by modern humans hunting on a much larger scale than Neanderthals ever had. Slaughtering mammoths in such staggering numbers provided modern humans a precious and abundant source of food, along with construction materials, bone and ivory for use in tools and art objects, hides for warmth and to create walls for the bone huts, and even fuel for fires. This would have given them a tremendous survival advantage, but what was the secret of their success?

One answer may be that by this time humans had developed improved weapons—light, easy-to-carry spears that could be thrown at a prey animal from a distance. Neanderthals did not have long-range spears; their primary hunting strategy was to ambush prey at close range and beat it to death with clubs—if they weren't themselves killed in the encounter.

But in her 2015 book *The Invaders,* Shipman suggests that a second innovation may have given humans a crucial advantage over their competitors. That innovation, she proposes, was dogs.

A WOLF CALLED ROMEO

Wild wolves are extremely wary of humans —so much so that it's rare for people to spot a wolf, even in areas they're known to inhabit. If they do encounter a human, wolves will almost always run away. A long history of human persecution makes this a reasonable response on the part of the wolf; another likely factor, according to the wolf biologist L. David Mech, is that humans' upright posture is unlike wolves' other prey and similar to some postures of bears, which wolves usually avoid.

Tireless and skillful predators, adult wolves necessarily spend many of their waking hours tracking their next meal, which means that in areas where humans and wolves live in close proximity, livestock and pets can be at risk. But there are exceptions. A wild wolf people called Romeo, who lived on the edge of suburban Juneau, Alaska, for over six years beginning in the winter of 2003, gave the many residents and

The young black male wolf dubbed Romeo by a local community of admirers in suburban Juneau, Alaska, was unafraid to come very close to humans and their dogs. He even enjoyed playing with some of the dogs.

their dogs who came to know him a close-up experience of the sort of human-friendly wolves who may have first dared approach our Paleolithic ancestors.

As recounted in his 2014 book *A Wolf Called Romeo*, wildlife photographer and author Nick Jans first saw the large black male wolf on the frozen lake outside his house. The animal was young and seemed solitary, rare for a wolf. He proved to be remarkably calm and unafraid in the company of Jans and other local people and their many pet dogs, who often gathered on the lake in winter to socialize and play. In fact, the wolf seemed downright lonely and eager for canine companionship, playing and even flirting with Jans's female Labrador retriever dog and others. It was that behavior that prompted Jans's wife to call the wolf Romeo, and the name stuck. He was believed to be the adolescent son of a female wolf who'd been killed by a taxicab in the area the previous spring, and he seemed to be without a wolf pack of his own.

For six winters he came and went on his own time, never asking for or receiving anything except companionship from the human and canine residents, many of whom forged close and enduring relationships with the wolf.

Romeo was unusual but not unique in his acceptance of and attraction to people, but his generally nonaggressive and playful approach to the people's domesticated dogs was rare for a wild wolf. As Jans, who has spent years around wolves, explained, "Wolves are like dogs, in that they all have different personalities. Some are more cautious or fearful than others. But this wolf was downright relaxed and tolerant from the start, as if he had dropped out of the sky like a unicorn."

In the end, Romeo met a tragic end at the

hands of humans, like so many of his kind have throughout history. By then, he was estimated to be at least eight years old, nearly three times the average lifespan of a wolf in the wild. "The amazing thing," said Jans, "was Romeo's understanding. It wasn't just our understanding and tolerance. It was a combination of his and ours and the dogs'. We were these three different creatures working out how to get along harmoniously. And we did."

In the days after first coming into contact with Nick Jans and his dogs, Romeo would sometimes be seen waiting outside their home early in the morning. Although he never tried to come any closer to the house, he seemed to long for a chance to spend time with the dogs, and took both humans and animals in stride—very unusual behavior for a wild wolf.

If it's true that some wolves were beginning domestication as early as thirty-six thousand years ago, then such transitional wolf-dogs were clearly associating in some way with early humans during the period when they shared territory with Neanderthals and competed with them for survival. There's no fossil evidence that Neanderthals had dogs or partly domesticated wolves, as humans did.

Shipman suggests we might think of these early dogs as "living tools"—as important as any tool humans ever invented. These were large, sturdy dogs; they could have been used to transport portions of mammoth carcasses and other large prey to human campsites. If these wolf-dogs lived with or near humans—in effect becoming part of the human "pack," as some fossil evidence suggests—they would naturally have guarded valuable meat supplies from intruders, including roving packs of their own wild wolf cousins. And this newer, friendlier kind of wolf may have provided companionship and warmth, along with protection; as the association grew stronger, wolves and wolf-dogs may have even taken on a spiritual role for the humans who adopted them.

Perforations in many of the earliest dog skulls, as well as the pierced canid teeth humans wore as jewelry and other evidence of ritual practices involving these first dogs, suggest that the first domesticated animal in the world was profoundly important to humans from the very beginning, on many levels. In these ancient artifacts paleontologists can trace the beginnings of a uniquely intimate relationship that led, much later, to the widespread practice of combined dog-human burials, beginning with the Bonn-Oberkassel dog carefully laid to rest with human companions fourteen thousand years ago, and then at other sites found all over the world.

Neanderthals also buried their dead, but no known Neanderthal burial sites have been found to contain the bones of dogs. As far as scientists can tell, domesticated wolves were not part of Neanderthal life, as they were for our own ancestors.

Domestication has profound implications for both humans and those relatively few species we've selected to add to our extended human tribe. It turns out that the animals and plants we've domesticated have changed *us,* just as much as we've changed *them.* For example, genetic alterations had to occur for adult humans to be capable of digesting milk, and this very mutation arose in human populations only after they had domesticated cattle, beginning a little more than ten thousand years ago. Since dogs are universally acknowledged to be the original domesticated species, we might expect to find that they have changed us, too. And this leads to another big what-if question. What if, in developing a domestic dog from a wild wolf, early humans unwittingly changed their own bodies and minds at least as much as they changed the minds and bodies of the wolves who became their dogs?

One tantalizing possible connection between humans and

dogs that Pat Shipman has proposed involves a unique feature of human anatomy—the whites of our eyes. Modern humans are the only surviving primates in the world to have highly visible white sclerae, which surround the colored irises of our eyes. Is it only coincidence that none of the other apes pays as much attention to the gaze of an eye as humans do? Researchers think this evolutionary adaptation in humans may have served to enhance the effectiveness of gaze signals as a form of human-to-human communication.

The direction in which we look tells those who can read this signal something about our intentions. And here's where dogs come in: it turns out that dogs can follow the human gaze, too, and they're very good at it—much better than wolves (who can follow the human gaze easily but most often choose not to do so, interpreting direct eye contact as a challenge). Tellingly, dogs also understand our gaze far better than our closest relative in the animal kingdom, the chimpanzee.

So why did modern humans evolve the white sclera, and when did it first develop? We don't yet have the answer to the latter question, but dogs' innate ability to read the human gaze suggests, to Shipman, something remarkable: in domesticating dogs, humans may have inadvertently evolved another feature that makes us unique among primates. At the same time, dogs developed an innate and universal interest in interpreting the human gaze. This tiny change was huge, enabling us to communicate much more effectively with our dogs—protectors,

Human eyes, with white sclera surrounding the pupils, give a clear signal of intent to those who are able to read it, including other humans and dogs.

Chimpanzee eyes are much harder to read than human eyes, and chimps are not as inclined to follow the direction of a human gaze as dogs are.

Siberian husky dogs often have blue eyes, which can be unusually expressive.

companions, and indispensable hunting partners—as well as with our fellow humans.

Imagine the Paleolithic hunter, crouched in the shadow of boulders or bushes, watching a browsing herd of reindeer. His two wolflike dogs sit silently at his feet, eyes upturned and fastened on the eyes of the man, then following the man's gaze to fix on a single grazing deer. Suddenly, silently, the man springs forward, winding back his right arm to throw a long-handled spear. But the dogs get to the bewildered prey first, startling it with loud barking and dancing around it with snapping jaws while the rest of the reindeer herd scatters in panic. The hunter takes aim and the spear brings down the animal, who dies instantly as the sharp-pointed tip pierces its heart.

Dogs' genetic makeup is nearly identical to that of wolves, but they make their living in a dramatically different way. No matter where dogs live, what their appearance is, or what else they do, they always live in close association with people. Or as Shipman says, "A dog is a wolf that acts like a dog and relates to people." Experiments have shown that even wolves and dogs exposed to human contact from birth grow up to have very different relationships and attitudes toward humans. In essence, dogs are intensely interested in people, and wolves are not. And because communication with humans is so fundamental to being a dog, Shipman reasons, "having a highly visible direction of gaze would have been a big advantage in hunting cooperatively with wolf-dogs," as well as with fellow humans.

Domestic dogs not only share the wolf's inborn ability to communicate with their pack members through their gaze, but they also gaze at humans for twice as long, on average, as wolves do. As experiments have shown, human infants, too, follow the human gaze better than wolves do; they also begin about as early in life and do it as well as domestic dogs. In test after test, dogs look to humans for guidance, copy human actions, and follow human gestures and gazes, while wolves do not. More than anything, this is what makes a dog a dog. If Shipman is correct in her hunch, our gaze and its communicative value may also be part of what made us human and saved us from the fate of Neanderthals—extinction.

Shipman's idea is, as she readily concedes, purely speculative for now. It's clearly in the category of *what if*. But what if a genetic basis for white sclerae is identified, as it almost certainly will be, and what if the random mutation for that trait occurred more often among modern humans than among Neanderthals? Shipman's hypothesis is that this feature could have enhanced communication between humans and dogs just as it did among humans. It would have facilitated the domestication of wolves. If Neanderthals *lacked* this mutation, they may have been unable to make the great leap to the domestication of wolves. Further analysis of Neanderthal DNA may someday give us the answer to that question, among many others.

If Shipman is correct, the whites of our eyes may have been one of many tiny, random mutations that have had huge consequences for our species—a trait peculiar to humans that co-evolved with dogs' powerful impulse to follow our unique gaze.

We have no way of knowing what Paleolithic humans who would become the first dog people, or wolves whose offspring would become dogs, were thinking. It all happened thousands of years ago, and thoughts leave no trace in the fossil record. But in the last few years, scientists studying dog evolution and genetics with new tools have brought us much closer to understanding how, where, and even approximately when our two species must have forged the first crucial bonds. One big question remains: Why? Was it a mutual attraction from the first, or did one of the two predatory species make the first move?

Eurasian humans of the late Upper Paleolithic era (about forty thousand to ten thousand years ago) lived in hunter-gatherer bands that were probably not much more civilized than the packs of wild wolves skulking around them, beyond having some rudimentary tools, hands to make and use them, and some form of spoken language.

Not only had they never conceived of domesticating any other animal, but they would not repeat the process with another species for a long time, domesticating sheep and goats only about eleven thousand years ago. So it's remarkable that this happened at all.

Before a wolf became the first dog, humans had not shown much tolerance for carnivorous competitors. Soon after their arrival in Europe, *Homo sapiens* had immediately set about wiping out every other large carnivore around, from saber-toothed cats to giant hyenas, while also decimating most of the large prey populations. It's curious, then, that wolves survived. While fossil evidence shows that humans killed some wolves, it also shows that they formed an alliance with others.

Why partner with wolves? They would certainly be expensive partners to keep. Even if joining with wolves could result in more successful hunting for early humans, would that be enough to make up for having to share precious protein with packs of voracious competitors? And wolves could make a meal of humans just as easily as they could of reindeer. If wolves killed a reindeer or a horse, they wouldn't share their kill with any wolf outside their pack, and they would not hesitate to attack anyone who tried to take away their hard-won meal—including humans. Why would early humans, who already lived perilous lives, choose to take such a risk? Perhaps it was the wolves who chose to take advantage of humans' hunting successes, positioning themselves to grab whatever leftovers they could.

A pair of very young gray wolf pups in a forest in Bavaria, Germany. It's easy to imagine the impulse of Paleolithic people to adopt such appealing pups as pets.

It could be that our Paleolithic ancestors sensed immediately that friendly wolves could be useful, but utility may not have been their sole motivation. Not to be discounted in the human-directed domestication scenario is the cuteness factor. Humans just seem to have a powerful inborn tendency to adopt other animals—especially baby animals—and raise them. We are the only species that does this on a large scale, and we do it a lot. Pets have been part of human culture since at least fourteen thousand years ago; the earliest dog-human burials provide clear evidence of the special bond between humans and dogs. It's possible that the impulse to keep wolf pups as pets, with no more utilitarian purpose in mind, was the one crucial motivation that first led humans to bring them into their lives. Pets—especially dogs—are still kept by people in all kinds of cultures all over the world, including modern hunter-gatherer bands still living much as our Paleolithic ancestors did.

But however the wolves first came into their caves and camps, it was humans who would have controlled which wolves stayed. Those who were aggressive would have been killed or driven away, and those who were very timid would never have approached in the first place. It was only wolves who were both friendly and bold who would have been tolerated, welcomed into the human fold, and allowed to breed.

With that, the stage was set for domestication to begin.

But what is domestication? And how is it different from simply taming a wild animal? A wild animal is a species that evolved in the wild, with a physiology, a mental capacity, and instincts best suited to the environment it evolved in. An individual wild animal can become *tamed* (conditioned to be more docile and submissive to humans), but it cannot become domesticated. Domestication occurs not in one animal but in a population of a species. Domestication is a process whereby humans have structurally, physiologically, and behaviorally modified certain species of animals by maintaining them in or near human habitation and by breeding those who seem best suited for various human objectives. Once a species has become domesticated, those modified traits are passed down to succeeding generations.

The first wild wolves to successfully live with or near humans had to become, to some extent, tame. Taming is the deliberate, human-directed process of training an animal against its initially wild or natural instincts to avoid (or attack) humans, so that instead the animal learns to tolerate them and even to seek out their company. Just as the offspring of a tame wolf, for example, will not be born tame because its mother was tame, the offspring of a domesticated dog will not be born wild, because tameness has become encoded in its genetic makeup.

In the late 1950s, a Russian geneticist named Dmitry Belyaev began a secret experiment that had an unexpected result. This result profoundly affected how evolutionary biologists understand domestication, and particularly the first domestication, which transformed wolves into dogs.

This was a dangerous time in Stalinist Russia for scientists who believed in Mendel's principles of genetic inheritance.

Those principles ran directly counter to the theories of an agronomist named Trofim Lysenko, who was a darling of the Soviet Communist Party. Belyaev had studied Mendel's ideas, and he suspected they might explain the confounding differences in anatomy, physiology, and behavior between domestic dogs and wolves.

The "silver fox experiment," still ongoing in Novosibirsk, Russia, today, began with wild foxes raised in captivity. They were selectively bred, generation after generation, based not on

As shown by Belyaev's long-running (and still ongoing) study, wild foxes selectively bred over generations for the trait of tameness alone will not only begin acting more like dogs than like wild foxes, but also begin to take on a doglike appearance, as does this eight-week-old domesticated silver fox.

At the Institute of Cytology and Genetics in Novosibirsk, Russia, a silver fox from a line never selectively bred for tameness displays fear and aggression at the approach of people. This captive wild fox is unchanged in either appearance or behavior from its fully wild relatives.

any details of their appearance, but on one factor only: the wild foxes who were least aggressive toward their human handlers—who permitted them to come near or even approached them with curiosity—were allowed to breed, but the foxes who snapped and snarled and cowered in the corners of their cages at the approach of a human were not.

Within just twenty generations, the result was a population of doglike foxes, who wagged their tails and licked the hands and faces of their human handlers. Surprisingly, in the same amount of time, these tame foxes had also started to *look* more like dogs!

Their skulls had become smaller and wider, their snouts shorter, teeth smaller, ears floppier, fur splotchier, and tails curlier. This was the first proof that selecting for less aggression would bring with it the side effect of more juvenile physical and behavioral traits.

The results of the silver fox experiment explained much about dogs. Basically, they revealed that all dogs are kids who never grow up.

The Siberian silver foxes purposely domesticated by Belyaev were selected for a single trait—tameness. But tameness brought with it a whole host of unexpected changes, including making the foxes more social. Could selection for tameness alone also have produced the superior social cognition of dogs?

Tests have shown that Belyaev's fox-dog puppies respond to human pointing gestures in the same way that domestic dog puppies do but that wild fox puppies do not. Selected and bred for tameness alone, neither handled more than nor treated differently from the wilder individuals, these foxes have evolved the same ability to follow and interpret the gestures of humans that are universal in domestic dogs. This ability to understand human social signals is what defines the dog and separates him from his wild canine cousins.

PETER PANS OF
THE CANINE FAMILY

At the time that purebred dogs were being developed, breeders had little understanding of *how* they were creating such wildly divergent canine sizes and shapes, beyond the simple process of breeding similar animals to one another. And as artificial selection came to define the shape of purebred dogs, some traits that would have been fatal in nature were not only *allowed* to be passed down to future generations of dogs, they were encouraged.

Now that scientists have cracked open the canine genetic code, they've discovered that a very small number of changes in the canine genome account for all of the vast differences in size and shape among breeds. The difference between a dachshund's small body and a Rottweiler's massive one is determined by the sequence of a single gene, as are the dachshund's stumpy legs as opposed to the long, sleek limbs of the grey-hound.

These minute sequences of genes control the transformation of juvenile dogs into their adult form, just as they transform soft, round-bodied, large-eyed wolf pups into the very different shape of adult wolves. Some of these genes also switch on adult wolf behavior, so that friendly, playful wolf pups become wary of humans and less playful in adulthood.

Compared with wolves, most adult dogs retain many juvenile characteristics even as they mature —as with Belyaev's domesticated foxes. This is called neoteny and most domesticated animals exhibit it to at least some degree. Juvenile features in dogs are inherently appealing to humans, just as juvenile features in human babies warm our hearts. A dog who looks more like a puppy than an adult wolf is clearly more heartwarming —and less threatening—to human caretakers. It's little wonder that humans chose to override the natural wolfishness of their earliest dogs as they realized they had the power to dramatically shape the evolution of the entire canine race.

Among the hundreds of modern dog breeds that emerged from the Victorian dog fancy,

Short-legged dachshunds charge down a track as enthusiastically as racing greyhounds at a festival in Rathdrum, Idaho.

certain genes that control the timing and rate of physical development are switched off, in whole or in part. So, for example, one breed may have a normal body size but very short legs (think dachshunds or corgis); another may have a large, adult-wolf-size body, but also a broad snout, flopped-over ears, and a tail that curves over the back instead of hanging straight down (Great Dane, Labrador retriever). Different breeds retain some puppy-like traits but not others. Most retain the cuteness factor that endears them to humans, but some breeds grow to be bigger than the largest wolf, and others never grow larger than a newborn pup. All domestic dogs mature sexually at an earlier age than wolves, another difference that biologists call paedomorphism, but many remain puppies at heart all their lives.

WRITTEN IN THE GENES

Reading the emotions of dogs is surprisingly easy for most people. Ollie is a trained search-and-rescue dog of mixed breeding whose entire expression here seems to communicate that he's happy, relaxed, and friendly.

U ntil recently, everything that was known about the origin of dogs came from fossils. Fossil bones and teeth, like pigments and ash residue on cave walls, can be approximately dated by means of radiocarbon analysis. But to

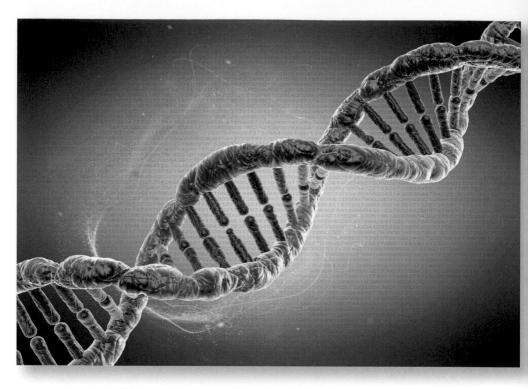

The DNA molecule, showing its double helix structure.

use this technique, the fossils must be found in the first place, and no one can say how many are still buried in the earth, undiscovered for now. Large gaps in the fossil record leave scientists with big questions about the evolution of any species or culture.

Cue the geneticists.

Genetics is the study of how traits are passed down from parents to offspring through DNA, the genetic code that is the blueprint of life. In the years since Mendel first discovered the basic principles of genetics in the 1860s, the science of molecular biology—the means by which scientists are able to study genes directly—has advanced beyond anything that Mendel or his contemporary Charles Darwin could have imagined. It began with the microscope, which made it possible, for the very first time, to observe life at the cellular and molecular levels.

Molecular biology revolutionized medicine and biochemistry as well as making possible the modern field of evolutionary biology. Once microbiologists gained the ability to analyze genes that could be extracted from fossil dogs and wolves and compare them with the animals' modern counterparts around the world, paleontology and molecular biology became closely linked in a fast-changing quest to trace the dog-human relationship from its earliest roots. It's through dramatic advances in the science of genetics over the past two decades that evolutionary biologists, paleontologists, and molecular biologists have begun accumulating evidence of the long, complicated journey of modern dogs from their beginnings as wild wolves.

When Darwin outlined his theory of evolution by natural selection, he knew that dogs represented an important piece of the puzzle, but he couldn't explain exactly how natural selection could have resulted in such a range of wildly different-looking animals in a single species. It would be nearly 150 years before that question could begin to be scientifically addressed with the first sequencing of a complete dog genome (that of a female boxer named Tasha) in 2005 — just two years after the first complete human genome had been published. By comparing this dog genome with the similarly deciphered genomes of modern gray wolves, geneticists were finally able to confirm that all dogs are descended from wolves, and not from wolves and several other canid species as Darwin had suspected.

But that was just the beginning.

By tracing genetic mutations back through time, comparing modern dogs and wolves with fossil remains, scientists are beginning to get a much clearer idea of when some wolves first diverged to become the earliest dogs, and even some clues as to where it happened. This has sparked a radical rethinking of dog domestication, but it has not settled all the questions. Proponents of the self-domestication theory contend that friendlier wolves were motivated to approach the human predator because of garbage dumps on the edge of human settlements. But if dogs were showing signs of domestication as early as the Goyet dog, thirty-six thousand years ago, there were no garbage dumps then. There were no permanent settlements and no agriculture; humans continued their nomadic, hunter-gatherer ways in Europe for at least another twenty-five thousand years. Some scientists even argue that it may have been the successful domestication of dogs that gave hunter-gatherers the idea, much later, to domesticate plants and other animals for greater food security.

Robert Wayne, an evolutionary biologist, geneticist, and leading dog/wolf researcher at the University of California, Los Angeles, has been in the forefront of the scientific rethinking of dog domestication. His work on the wolf genome provided some of the earliest clear evidence of the direct relationship between dogs and wolves. His latest findings reveal more. They suggest that the first dogs evolved not from any line of wolf currently alive in the world, but from a now-extinct group of European wolves. That happened, he says, sometime between about thirty-two thousand and eighteen thousand years ago, after these ancient wolves began growing closer and closer to human hunter-gatherers.

More answers are on the way. Researchers are now able to extract DNA from ancient wolf and dog fossils and compare it in a more detailed way than ever before with DNA from modern dog breeds and wolves. At the same time, early results have revealed just how confusing trying to trace the genetic lineage of domestic dogs will be. This is because newly domesticated dogs continued to breed with wild wolves after domestication, and also because domestication probably happened in several locations and at different times, with some early dog lines going extinct. Besides, humans are a restless species, and we've taken our beloved dogs with us whenever we moved. Once wolves became dogs, they began crisscrossing the globe with their wandering human companions, traveling to places far from their geographic origins.

In a 2002 study, evolutionary biologist Jennifer Leonard analyzed a group of North American dog fossils from animals who lived between 1450 and 1675 A.D., well before the first Europeans viewed Alaska in 1741. This meant they had to be native to America, but the question of their ancestry remained unsolved. At the time of the study, the precise locations where dog domestication began were even more of a mystery than they are today. Were these all-American dogs descended from North American gray wolves once domesticated by Native Americans? Only the DNA from their bones would tell. So the genetic material was extracted and analyzed, along with that from the bones of other dogs from archaeological sites in Mexico, Peru, and Bolivia that predated the arrival of Columbus.

The results were a big surprise. All of these American dogs were descended from gray wolves native to Europe and Asia; they bore no genetic relationship to the indigenous North American wolf at all. They likely came from various lineages of Asian dogs who had traveled far from their origins, just as Eurasian humans had done. From that time forward, dogs and the people who would give rise to Native American populations migrated across the whole of North, Central, and South America.

For a major study published in the journal *Science* in late 2013, Robert Wayne's team studied the DNA of ten ancient fossils with wolflike traits and eight doglike fossils from Europe, dating from thirty-two thousand to nineteen thousand years ago. The researchers found that the domestic dogs grouped genetically with ancient wolves or modern dogs from Europe, and not with wolves found anywhere else in the world or even with modern European wolves.

The explosion of new research in this field is still frustratingly (or intriguingly) inconclusive, as different researchers work to piece it together, tracing the history of dogs bit by genetic bit. More recent studies suggest that wolves may have evolved not in any one place, but in two — Asia and Europe. According to this scenario, separate domestication events involving different people and different wolves contributed to the complicated lineage of dogs.

While geneticists try to understand the twisting trail of ancient dogs, ancient hominid DNA is also being studied. In December 2013 international teams of scientists published their analysis of the full Neanderthal genome, extracted from a 130,000-year-old toe bone found in a Siberian cave. This kind of information is beginning to answer the most basic questions about how our own species and that of the Neanderthals diverged from a common African ancestor. Similar revelations about how dogs diverged from wolves are close at hand with the coming unveiling of the full genome extracted from ancient dog fossils.

What scientists are discovering in the genes of ancient and modern dogs and humans is just how closely our two species have evolved in parallel since the first wolves moved in to stay. John Bradshaw is a biologist and dog researcher based at the Anthrozoology Institute of England's University of Bristol, and he has a hunch about those friendly wolves. He thinks the wolves who became dogs were already preadapted to get along with humans. No one would have known this, of course, if the two species had not happened to meet along the trail. But somehow, both these particular presocialized wolves and early humans recognized a certain affinity. As Bradshaw writes in his 2012 book, *In Defence of Dogs,* "It is entirely possible that some accident of genetics—some sort of mutation—gave a few wolves the ability to socialize to two species simultaneously, to direct their social behavior to mankind and other wolves," while still breeding with their own species. This capacity for the dog to adopt a dual identity—part human and part wolf—is essential in accounting for the transition from primitive pet to truly domesticated animal.

If it's true, as Bradshaw believes, that those wolves possessed an accidental capacity to become "part human," is it equally true that the first humans to domesticate dogs, in some sense, became part wolf? This poetic and fanciful idea begins to make scientific sense on a genetic level the more we learn about parallel mutations in the genes of humans and dogs over the thousands of years that our species have traveled and lived together.

Before there were dogs, there were bold and curious wolves, and from them sprang the earliest protodogs. These wild canids, living in a time when *all* animals, including humans, were wild, nevertheless possessed unusual social skills that enabled them to approach and interact with humans in a whole new way. They still *looked* a great deal like wolves, with a fairly uniform appearance, probably resembling a modern Siberian husky but supersize—similar in height and weight to today's largest German shepherd dogs. Over time, domestication began to change both the appearance and the behavior of these first dogs, but the close interspecies partnership also changed *humans* in profound ways—even if most of those changes were not visible to the naked eye. What changed was the very essence of what it meant to be human, living in ever larger social groups of other humans and their dogs.

The great survival advantages of living with dogs made possible dramatic breakthroughs in human cultural expression, communication, and all forms of social interaction. It's no surprise that these advances coincided with the human transition from a perilous, energy-intensive hunter-gatherer existence to the beginnings of agricultural settlements and more complex social communities. Many paleoanthropologists agree that the well-known Australian Aboriginal expression "Dogs make us human," quite accurately reflects the shared ancestral history of humans and dogs.

But it was only with the new ability of scientists to identify the individual genes of whole organisms that we began to understand the extent to which our physical being was modified by our intimate association with dogs. Soon after coming together, the biology of both humans and wolves began to transform as their DNA evolved in parallel ways in response to their shared changed environment.

After dogs split from wolves, some of their genes began to shift in a whole new way. Some of these genetic mutations

—those that gave these ancient wolves a survival advantage—were passed along to succeeding generations. Scientists have been able to identify specific groups of modified genes and are beginning to understand how profoundly these small mutations have transformed the bodies and minds of dogs. In a groundbreaking 2013 study, canine geneticists compared the DNA of twelve gray wolves from around the world and sixty domestic dogs of fourteen different breeds, searching for small differences that may have shown up early in the evolution from wolf to dog. They focused on specific mutations that all dogs have and that wolves do not. Thirty-six genes from different regions of the genome were found to fit this picture. Nineteen of those genes play a role in brain development or function, and another group is known to influence how cells divide, a crucial factor in the development of cancers.

But researchers were most surprised by mutations they discovered that modify dogs' ability to digest starch and metabolize fats in their diet. At some as yet undetermined point in the distant past, humans also evolved this same digestive ability, allowing us to greatly expand the availability and diversity of our food supply—the same foods we now share with dogs.

Dogs, compared with wolves, carry extra copies of genes that convert starch into maltose, a carbohydrate that gets converted by the body into sugar. They also have mutations in another gene that aids in the digestion of sugars, and in a third gene that makes a protein that transports glucose, or sugar, from the gut into the bloodstream. This explains why most dogs are

Most dogs love bread, and thanks to gene mutations they've evolved
alongside humans, they can easily digest it. Gray wolves, though,
are primarily carnivorous and rarely eat starchy foods.

fond of treats such as bread and cookies, while wolves prefer a
mostly meat diet; dogs can digest such starchy foods, and wolves
can't digest them nearly as well.

If the dating of dog skull fossils to thirty-six thousand
years ago is correct, the process of domestication began before —
possibly *long* before — humans learned to cultivate plants. Dogs
are still carnivores, just like their wolf ancestors, but although
most prefer meat and other proteins, they'll happily snack on
pizza crusts or a muffin anytime. And their love of starchy foods,
we now know, goes back a long time; researchers determined

that starch-digesting mutations originated in dogs long before the development of most modern breeds.

Whenever these changes occurred, dogs had already adapted, at the fundamental level of their DNA, to a diet that included grains before agriculture began. So the starchy foods of early human farmers would have been an easy-to-digest, tasty addition to the canine diet. And it was not just dogs who evolved the ability to digest starch; evolving right alongside them were early human agriculturists. Their genes changed to allow them to more easily digest starches with the rise of farming around ten thousand years ago in the Middle East. For both humans and dogs, this adaptation would have been hugely beneficial. Compared with the food choices of our hunter-gatherer ancestors who first invited friendly wolves to share in their mammoth meals, the new ability to digest starches and sugars would have greatly expanded the menu for all.

This is just one example of the process scientists call co-evolution; starch-digesting mutations are found in one of several groups of genes now known to have been evolving in a parallel way in both humans and dogs for thousands of years. The reason? Proximity. Living so closely together in a shared environment over time is thought to drive genetic changes. When closely interacting species, responding to shared environmental conditions, exert specific selective pressures on one another, a kind of conversation of adaptations can be set in motion. For example, different types of hummingbirds have evolved different beak shapes and sizes to match particular varieties of flowers that they pollinate; these plants have evolved flowers that attract the birds with conspicuous colors and shapes that perfectly accommodate the bird's beak as it drinks the nectar that sustains it.

Coevolution is one of several recognized patterns of evolution; another sometimes overlapping pattern is called convergence, a process by which unrelated species evolve similar traits in response to shared environmental pressures. Coevolution is often seen in nature, but selection of the very same gene in two unrelated species is rare. Selection of *many* mutated genes across species, like those being identified in the genes of humans and dogs, may be unique in the animal kingdom.

Is it unique? Until the genes of goats, sheep, cattle, horses, pigs, and other domesticated species have been sequenced and compared, researchers can't say for sure. But scientists studying the genomes of humans and dogs consider the parallels remarkable, if not entirely surprising. Since dogs have shared our living spaces for thousands of years longer than any other species, it makes sense that this ancient partnership is reflected in our genomes. And since domestication is often associated with large increases in population density and more crowded living conditions, researchers hypothesize that such crowding may account for the selective pressure that rewired the genes of both humans and their dogs.

Another major group of genetic mutations identified in dogs are those involved in how cells divide and replicate. Of these, one of the most interesting ones that scientists have identified is *Met proto-oncogene,* known to geneticists as MET. This mutation has been linked to cancer, but it also has another important function in the body: MET shapes wiring connections between neurons in the brain involved in social and emotional behavior. Researchers now believe that this mutation carries one of the strongest genetic risks for autism, an increasingly diagnosed human developmental disorder that causes difficulties with social interaction and verbal and nonverbal communication.

Whether dogs can suffer from humanlike autism is not yet known, but some dogs exhibit symptoms of obsessive-compulsive disorder (OCD), a condition thought to be related to autism. These dogs engage in repetitive, seemingly involuntary behaviors such as licking their paws or chasing their tails for hours on end. Knowing that dogs share the MET mutation with humans, some researchers are beginning to look at dog DNA to better understand autism on a genetic level. Because the full dog genome is a bit shorter and less complex than the human version, such studies (for which researchers obtain the dogs' DNA through simple swabs of the inner cheek and saliva) are much easier to carry out than similar studies on humans.

Why would a gene mutation like MET that contributes to cancer, autism, and OCD in both humans and dogs have evolved in the first place? It might seem to contradict the very notion of survival of the fittest. The short answer is that genetics is complicated and still incompletely understood. But scientists do know that many genes are active in different parts of the body and have more than one function. One of these functions may boost the survival of an organism, while another is detrimental to it. But if the advantage outweighs the negative effect, that particular gene sequence can still be "selected." In the case of MET, geneticists speculate that the mutation may have evolved as a defense against early cancers in both humans and dogs, or it may have been crucial for the necessary emergence of sociable people and dogs under pressure from increased crowding.

For now there are still more questions than answers, but the questions point to fascinating directions for future research. Dogs not only get cancer at a rate similar to that of humans (and significantly higher than cats and other pets), but they also tend to get the same *kinds* of cancer that plague human populations. Shared diet and lifestyle may account for this, but research is ongoing.

Some of the most intriguing genes that humans and dogs share are those involved with brain function. We already know that both modern dogs and modern humans have shrunken brains. We know this because researchers have looked at endocasts —molds of the brain created from imprints made of the inside of fossil skulls. In 2010, while researching the skull of a

Cro-Magnon man, scientists first discovered that the brain of our ancient ancestor was significantly larger than the brains of humans today.

Alarming as this may sound, evolutionary biologists recognize it as a universal signature of domestication. Domestic species across the board, from pigs to chickens to rats, have brains that are smaller, relative to their body size, than their wild counterparts. Dogs' brains are about 15 percent smaller than those of wolves. And at the same time that dogs' brains were shrinking, our human brains were shrinking too—by some 10 to 30 percent compared with the brains of our ancestors ten thousand years ago! It would be wrong to conclude that modern humans, with all of our cultural and technological accomplishments, are less intelligent than ancient humans were, and it would be equally wrong to suppose that dogs are less intelligent than their ancient wolf ancestors. But in both cases, their intelligence is of a different sort.

Humans and dogs, living so closely together over time, evolved specialized brain capacities that complemented one another perfectly. Humans lost a percentage of brain regions that formerly handled sensory processing (especially the sense of smell) and reactions, as more of these functions were taken over by domesticated dogs. But they retained the well-developed frontal lobes that govern higher mental processes such as reasoning, planning, and memory. Dogs may have lost some problem-solving skills once they began relying on humans for dinner, but they kept their more highly developed abilities to detect sensory input such as smells and sounds, as well as their finely tuned ability to read social cues and emotions. You might say that in the process, both humans and dogs became "smarter" despite losing a small percentage of their respective brain volumes.

To canine scientists, one of the most interesting genes found in dogs—but not in wolves—is called SLC6A4. This gene governs the level of a neurotransmitter (a chemical that transfers signals from one nerve cell in the brain to another) called serotonin. Serotonin is important because having too little in the brain can increase aggression; on the flip side, higher levels contribute to feelings of well-being and happiness. It can also have far-reaching effects on appetite, sleep, memory, and learning. But it's the influence of serotonin on the level of aggressive behavior that is especially relevant when it comes to domestication.

The earliest contacts between wolves and humans were surely risky for both. Aggressive wolves would have been killed or driven away by well-armed humans protecting hearth and home, and mellower wolves would be perceived as a lesser threat. For two predators coming face to face, friendliness might have been more important than strength.

Both human and wolf populations prospered and increased. But interacting in larger groups became more complicated. Under these circumstances, getting along with others would have been crucial for the survival of the group. Researchers think the SLC6A4 mutation could have been selected in both humans and these early dogs as a necessary adaptation to living in bigger crowds, since it lowered levels of aggression. Remarkably, our

Even working dogs need downtime. Wyatt and Ben, both search dogs, relax after a good time playing in fall leaves. The gene mutation SLC6A4 contributes to their happy relaxation by promoting the release of seratonin in their brains.

newly shared environment seems to have caused the same mutation in the brains of both humans and dogs.

In human brains, serotonin promotes bonding and trust; this mutation would have worked similarly in the brains of calmer, gentler wolves by increasing their serotonin levels, which would make taming a wild carnivore considerably less daunting for people who dared to try it. Because of this shared mutation, human antidepressants such as Prozac that work by regulating serotonin transport in the brain are as effective for dogs with OCD and other anxiety disorders as they are for human patients.

In the camps of the first humans to bring protodogs into their Ice Age living spaces, human and dog brains affected by the common SLC6A4 mutation would have been awash in serotonin. Some evolutionary biologists hypothesize that humans with the mutation would have been better equipped to facilitate cooperation and conflict avoidance as living conditions became more cramped, helping our own species to make the all-important transition from the culture of aggression and dominance that characterizes the social structure of other great apes to a culture of cooperation and communication that led to technological innovation, artistic expression, and the advancement of human civilization.

In this view, such genetically "advanced" humans would have succeeded in domesticating not only wild wolves but also, in a sense, themselves. Wolves with the same mutation in their brain chemistry, triggered by extended proximity to growing human populations, would have been prewired for domestication. Tracing the timing of such mutations in the genomes of both humans and dogs, and comparing it with the established fossil evidence of very early dogs, will reveal worlds about what makes us human and how dogs came to be our best friends.

People with the MET gene mutation may develop obsessive-compulsive disorder, but when a dog who inherits the same mutation develops a canine version of the condition, animal behaviorists diagnose "canine compulsive disorder." That's because the word "obsessive" describes the nature of thoughts, and none of us can know for sure what dogs are thinking.

Or can we?

Gregory Berns is a neuroscientist, a professor at Emory University, and, not incidentally, a lifelong dog guy. As a neurobiologist, he studies the cells of the nervous system and how they're organized into functional circuits that process information and mediate behavior. For more than twenty years, his professional interests have focused on understanding the neurobiological basis of individual preferences—how brain signals affect the decisions people make—a field now known as neuroeconomics. Researchers in this field use functional magnetic resonance imaging technology (fMRI) to measure the activity in key parts of the brain involved in decision making. Using this tool, scientists have linked the pattern of activity in the striatum, located in the human forebrain, with how people assess risk and reward. Understanding how this works has many practical applications—everything from understanding how people make decisions about investments to predicting the commercial success of popular songs. But after decades of using fMRI technology to study how the human brain works, Berns the dog lover was left with a vexing, unanswered question: what is my *dog* thinking?

After his family adopted Callie, a small, shy, mixed-breed terrier from a local animal shelter, Berns decided there was only one way to find out, and that was to use the MRI machine to scan his dog's brain, just as he had so many times before with human volunteers.

His colleagues said it couldn't be done.

The trouble was, Gregory Berns didn't just want to see inside his dog's brain; he wanted to watch it work. He wanted to visualize physical changes in the brain that happened when Callie thought about specific things that triggered emotions or perceived certain sights, smells, and sounds that promised a reward. This was theoretically possible, and well-proven with human subjects, using fMRI. The technique involves taking multiple pictures of the brain, in rapid-fire succession, to show which particular brain structures are active in real time. The structures light up as the subject thinks or processes sensory input.

From studies with human subjects, scientists already had a good idea of which brain regions are involved in certain kinds of thought and emotion. Though the brains of dogs look different in many ways, the basic components are equivalent. One of these areas is the caudate nucleus. This structure is found in the most ancient part of the brain, what's known as the reptilian brain, located at the base, near the brain stem. All mammals have it. In humans, it's the heart of our reward system. It fires when something unexpected occurs that indicates a good thing is about to happen.

Predicting what comes next is crucial for survival in all mammals, so it's a basic function of the brain in any mammal species. If the caudate nucleus operates in the same way in dogs as it does in humans, and if it could be observed by MRI

A WINDOW INTO THE CANINE BRAIN

Magnetic resonance imaging (MRI) uses a large, sophisticated machine to investigate the anatomy and function of the body by means of strong magnetic fields and radio waves. These record extremely detailed, multilayered, and three-dimensional images, which are then digitally processed. It's a painless, noninvasive procedure that uses no radiation. Since it was developed in the late 1970s, MRI has become an essential tool in both medical diagnosis and research, because it's often the best way to see inside the body without cutting it open. Functional magnetic resonance imaging (fMRI) is a neuroimaging procedure using MRI technology that measures brain activity by detecting associated changes in blood flow. This technique relies on the fact that cerebral blood flow and neuronal activation are coupled. When an area of the brain is in use, blood flow to that region increases.

There's just one catch, or rather two catches: one, the patient or subject must hold absolutely still inside the narrow, tubelike machine for up to an hour or more, depending on the procedure; and two, the machine makes continuous loud clanging, clicking, and banging noises that can be disturbing to many people.

Although MRI is very safe for patients, care must be taken to remove any kind of metal before a subject enters the scanner—otherwise the ultrapowerful magnets could cause iron-containing metal jewelry, internal implants such as pacemakers, or even tiny metal buttons, snaps, or threads in clothing to become overheated or distorted and even send them flying around the examination room as tiny projectiles. Ear-protecting headphones, often playing music to mask the noise, are usually worn by the patient, and some people even require sedatives to counter anxiety caused by having to remain absolutely still in such a confined, noisy space.

Beginning in the 1980s, MRI has also been used by veterinarians, since it offers the same advantages as it does for human patients. But for animals, general anesthesia is usually required to ensure that the patient or research subject will hold absolutely still during the procedure.

imaging, it would be possible to tell how a dog felt about something she knew was about to happen—a good first step in figuring out how the dog might be thinking and responding.

Gregory Berns realized that if he anesthetized Callie, her scan would tell him nothing that he wanted to know. But how could he get her to willingly go into the machine and hold absolutely still long enough to see her brain in action? She was, after all, a dog.

The answer, as it turned out, was hot dogs. *Lots* of hot dogs, along with patient training that included many practice sessions in a mock MRI coil Berns built in his living room, before moving on to the real scanner. It also included many trial runs of perfecting the ear muffs needed to protect sensitive canine hearing from the racket going on inside an MRI machine. But eventually, both Callie and another dog, a border collie named McKenzie, became not only willing to enter and lie motionless in the scanner, but eager to do it. With ear muffs wrapped securely around their heads, and snouts resting motionless on a special support the researchers placed inside the scanner, the dogs would hold still for up to thirty seconds at a time—long enough to get good-quality images.

This was the beginning of what came to be known as the Dog Project.

After those first sessions in the scanner proved successful, Callie and McKenzie were trained to recognize two hand signals. One meant that a bit of hot dog was coming, and the other meant there would be no hot dog. The handler would stand in front of the scanner, within the dog's line of sight, giving these hand signals. As expected, the fMRI clearly showed responses in the caudate nucleus to the "reward" signal and not to the "no reward" sign.

After that, the researchers began to devise more complex tests of the dogs' thought processes. A second experiment tested their responses to scents—their own scent, that of both familiar and strange humans, and of familiar and strange dogs. This was a way to separate the simple physical response to food rewards from an emotional response to a social reward. By comparing relative levels of activity in the caudate nucleus, it was possible to tell how much of a dog's motivation is a response to food and how much is due to social interaction with a human or with another member of her own species.

The question was, do dogs love us for ourselves or just for the treats we give them? And do they recognize us and respond differently to us than to all the strange humans they encounter? The results so far—a surprise to no one who has a dog—suggest that they can clearly tell the difference, and that their emotional responses are pretty much the same as our own would be. They experience pleasure, maybe even joy, in the presence of their own kind and of the people with whom they are bonded.

"Gazing into our dogs' brains," Berns has written, "is like a portal back in time. We now have the tools to see how they see us. We can see the things activating in their heads that our hominid ancestors selected from the dogs' wolf brethren. And now we can see it from the dog's perspective."

The idea that dogs may share with humans an ability to empathize with others, and to figure out what another creature, even one of another species, is thinking—what psychologists call theory of mind—is one that dog lovers have long taken for granted but that science is only recently beginning to acknowl-

edge. A growing number of studies involving both neuroimaging and behavioral experiments have shown that dogs have a high capacity for empathy. Not only can they figure out what humans think, they may also feel what humans feel. It's possible that dogs are unique in this interspecies social

Callie and her brain. And her Kong toy!

intelligence; the brain data from these MRI experiments suggest to Berns that they are.

Since those first, groundbreaking trials with Callie and McKenzie, dozens more dogs and their owners have volunteered to join the Dog Project. Many have successfully completed basic training in the scanner, and future trials are expected to shed light on a whole array of previously unanswerable questions: Do dogs truly have empathy for the emotional states of other dogs? What about for humans they know and those they don't? How much language do they understand? Do our dogs miss us when we're gone? Do they have any true sense of the passage of time, or an ability to form memories of specific events in the past that they can later recall? Are there differences in empathy and social cognition among different breeds of dogs? If, for example, one breed shows more of an empathic response to humans than another, will the more empathic dog be more successful as a therapy or service dog?

Another group of researchers, at the Institute of Cognitive Neuroscience and Psychology in Budapest, Hungary, has also

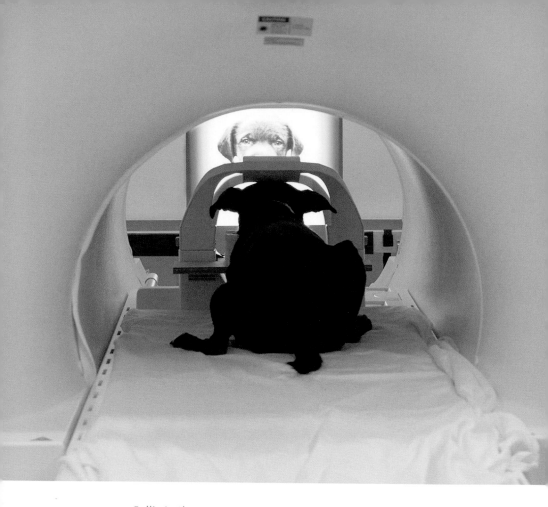

Callie in the scanner, viewing an image of a dog while the
scanner records how her brain responds to this cue.

trained dogs to participate in MRI studies of their brains, and
their findings help to explain an experience most dog people
know well: the very comforting presence of one's dog when a
person is sad, angry, or upset. Our dogs always seem to know
when we need a sloppy kiss, a nuzzle in the hair, or even an entire dog plopped onto our lap. It's not from any words we say to
them; even though the average dog can understand more than
one hundred words, this is hardly enough to form the basis of a

sophisticated, emotionally charged conversation. So how do they know when their human is feeling sad?

These scientists found that dogs have a small region in their brains devoted to deciphering emotions in dog and human voices. And what's more, this neural circuitry is located in the very same region, and seems to operate in the same way, as a corresponding voice-detection feature found in human brains!

Canadian researchers first identified the so-called voice area in the human brain in the late 1990s. Its function is not to process the meanings of words or sentences but to figure out the emotional information being conveyed along with the words. Not only does this patch of brain activate when people are identifying a speaker, it also interprets the mood of the speaker: angry, happy, silly, snarky, sad.

To test how the voice area in dogs compares, MRI-trained dogs were outfitted with headphones that played three types of sounds: human voices, dog voices, and random environmental noises such as a ringing phone or a hammer striking a nail. Then the scientists looked to see which parts of the dogs' brains responded to the sounds.

It was no big surprise that the brains of dogs responded most strongly to the voices of their own species—the barks, growls, and whines of other dogs. But it turned out that the canine voice recognition area was also sensitive to the emotional tones in human voices. The researchers found that these responses were very similar to corresponding human responses in previous studies. The same brain region was involved, and it lit up more

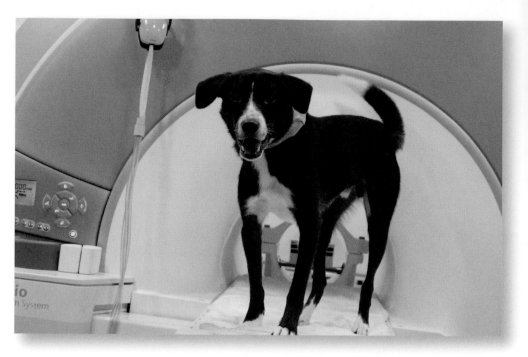

Huxley, looking happy after only his second time in the scanner.

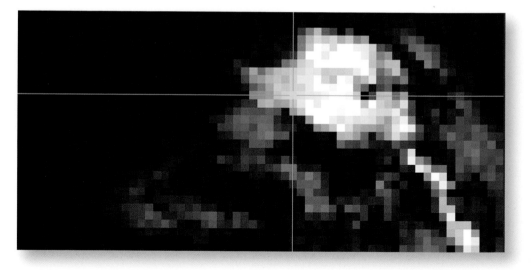

This image of Huxley in the scanner shows the first recorded result of activity in a dog's brain—in response to a hand signal indicating "hot dog"!

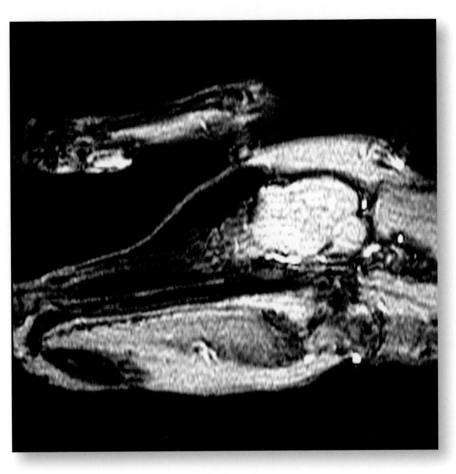

Huxley's brain.

strongly with positive, happy voices than with negative ones. (Is it possible that other animals—especially domestic ones—might respond similarly to the emotional content of human speech? Perhaps, but so far no one has devised such a test, and that may be the point. It's dogs, exquisitely responsive to the human voice and touch, who easily adapt to the unnatural demands of the MRI scanner.)

After identifying the active brain regions, scientists analyzed

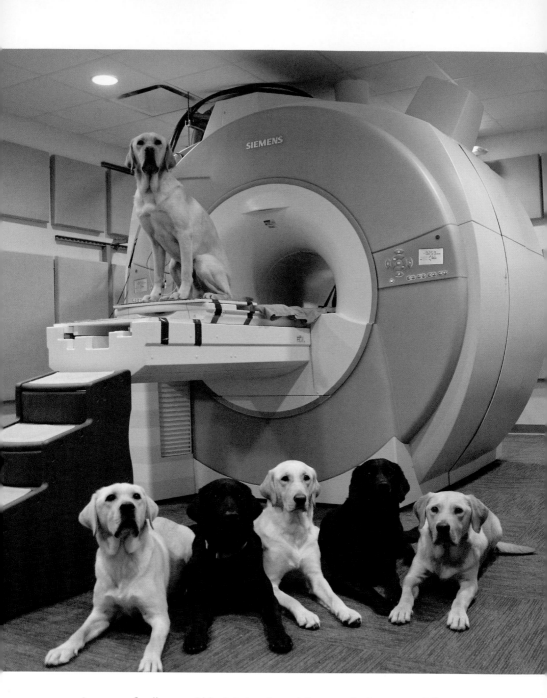

A group of yellow and black Labrador retrievers relaxing around the scanner on day two of their assignment. They seem to be enjoying the work.

what it is that alerts both humans and dogs to the difference between a happy voice and a sad one. For both species it was the
length and pitch of the tones. Just like us, dogs can instinctively
tell the difference between a happy laugh or bark and a sad moan
or whine. In a companion study, researchers established that humans can read a dog's mood in the very same way—from the
sound of the voice. They played about two hundred nonverbal
vocalizations of both dogs and humans to a group of Hungarian
human volunteers. These subjects were very good at correctly
interpreting the feelings behind both the human and the dog
voices; it seems that the same rules apply to both species. When
it comes to understanding emotions through the subtle differences in the pitch of a voice, we share a common language. That
language grew out of cooperative strategies that helped both humans and dogs become wildly successful species, and from the
deep emotional bond that developed along the way.

6

THE DOG ON THE COUCH: CANINE PSYCHOLOGISTS

Is this a guilty expression on Ben's face? It may be, but canine behavioral scientists caution against anthropomorphism when interpreting the feelings and behaviors of dogs.

Even after thousands of years of coevolution—after sharing our dinner and our beds with the descendants of wolves since the days of our Paleolithic ancestors—we still don't fully know dogs. Without a language to tell us what they may think or feel, dogs (like other nonhuman animals) are mysterious, their interior lives—if they have any—seemingly unknowable. Even with complex machines that can now reveal what parts of a dog's brain light up in response to a particular stimulus and how this compares with similar responses in the human brain, neuroscientists can't say with certainty how it feels to *be* a dog—how it feels to see the world through a dog's eyes or smell it through a dog's remarkable nose.

But just as we naturally want to understand what our human friends might be thinking, we really want (and sometimes *need*) to know what our canine friends are thinking and why they do the things they do. We can't simply ask them to explain themselves. Because we're so close to our dogs and because we see the world through human eyes, we're tempted to assume that their thoughts and motivations mirror our own, but do they? Canine cognitive scientists—known variously as cognitive ethologists, comparative evolutionary biologists, or canine behaviorists—are finally beginning to unravel the workings of the canine mind by using many of the same tools as those employed by human developmental psychologists.

After Darwin's broad musings in the mid-nineteenth century on the capacity of dogs to experience humanlike emotions, thoughts, and even a kind of morality, a brief flurry of speculation on this subject by other thinkers of his time followed. (Could dogs identify the social status of people just by smelling them? Perhaps! Since dogs can clearly understand words, could they be taught to read? Why not?)

In the early twentieth century, the American psychologist E. L. Thorndike built puzzle boxes and observed how different animals—cats, dogs, and chicks—figured out how to escape from them and receive a food reward in the bargain. His conclusion: animals learn strictly through simple associations, and any consideration of animal reason, insight, or consciousness is irrelevant and even misleading. His work and that of others—like the Russian physiologist I. P. Pavlov (known for his studies of conditioned reflexes in dogs) and two influential American psychologists, John. B. Watson and B. F. Skinner—ushered in a widespread belief in behaviorism that dominated scientific thinking on animal cognition and behavior for more than half a century. According to behaviorism, all animal behavior can be explained in terms of "conditioning," without appeal to thoughts or feelings. This

B. F. Skinner at Harvard University in 1964, presented his Skinner Box. With this apparatus, Skinner demonstrated his belief that animal cognition was a simple matter of operant conditioning. Brown lab rats learned by reinforcement with food rewards when they pressed a lever in the box.

way of thinking about animal intelligence remained popular until the latter part of the twentieth century, when scientific interest in how dogs learn fell off sharply.

The reason canine cognition was suddenly considered unworthy of scientific study was simple enough. Dogs were domesticated animals—artificial products of human meddling. Most animal researchers at the time believed that domestication dulled an animal's intelligence, simply because domesticated creatures no longer needed the same skills and intellect that had helped their wild cousins survive. Besides, studying domesticated animals seemed to contradict a basic premise of ethology, the branch of zoology so brilliantly exemplified by Darwin more than a hundred years earlier in his meticulous field studies of Galápagos finches and other wild species. Ethology is based on observing animal behavior not in an artificial lab but under natural conditions. So what was the "natural condition" of the dog? Curled up at the foot of a human's bed, it seemed, waiting for a daily scoop of kibble and a walk in the park. Nothing happening here, folks. Move along.

Only two research projects involving dog cognition were conducted between 1950 and 1995. One was a pioneering study by American researchers John Paul Scott and John L. Fuller. In their 1965 book *Genetics and the Social Behavior of the Dog*, based on a large and ambitious dog-breeding experiment they'd begun in 1947, Scott and Fuller proposed a number of parallels between human and dog cognition, but no one ever expanded on these findings. No one seemed to pay much attention at all.

It wasn't until the 1970s, with the gradual decline of behaviorism, that scientists resumed studying animal cognition in earnest. Initially their interest centered on nonhuman primates —monkeys and apes. Even if humans weren't the *only* thinking animals, the reasoning went, surely that distinction would be limited to our closest living relatives in the animal kingdom. They would be smarter than most animals, more like us. Smarter was better, and this scientific interest in brainpower eventually extended to other apparently intelligent animals such as crows and the mysterious, large-brained dolphin. Dogs, on the other hand, continued their long run of neglect by the scientific community.

This disinterest shifted dramatically beginning in about 1995, when two young researchers, working independently on opposite sides of the world, made the same startling discovery —that dogs might be among the *most* important species for cognitive scientists to consider.

A new generation of scientists would go far beyond Scott and Fuller's work by hypothesizing a behavioral convergence between humans and dogs. They discovered, almost by accident, something that had never before been demonstrated by cognitive scientists or evolutionary biologists: Among all nonhuman species on earth, *only dogs* are able to understand and communicate with humans in the same way that normal humans master at an early age. The way dogs learn from and interact with humans, they found, mirrors the ways children learn from and interact with their parents or other adults. These shared social and communicative skills between such seemingly unrelated species seem to represent a phenomenon known to evolutionary biologists as psychological convergence.

Convergence that takes the form of similar physical structures, such as fins or wings, is fairly common in the animal kingdom; convergence of the genes of dissimilar species, although remarkable, is a finding so new that scientists can't yet say how frequently it occurs. Psychological and behavioral convergence is believed to be quite rare, yet the researchers newly immersed in dog cognition were able to demonstrate just such a fundamental link between humans and dogs.

For these scientists, human-canine psychological convergence was an electrifying—and a groundbreaking, career-making—discovery.

Neither Brian Hare nor Ádám Miklósi had originally set out to study dog cognition. Hare, a self-described "dog guy" whose childhood best friend had, indeed, been his dog, Oreo, is now a professor of evolutionary anthropology at Duke University and founder of the Duke Canine Cognition Center. But back in 1995, he was an undergraduate student of anthropology and psychology at Emory University in Atlanta, working with Michael Tomasello, a highly regarded developmental psychologist who had been among the first scientists to show that normal human infants develop powerful, crucial social skills as early as nine months old. Even though it takes many more months for babies to begin using spoken language, these early, inborn social skills allow them to communicate with their mothers or other caregivers and to learn important information about the world.

Two of the most important skills that Tomasello identified were the natural ability and desire of infants to follow the gaze of another person, and soon after that, to also follow the pointing gestures of a parent or caregiver. In this way, infants begin to read the intentions of other people, an important first step in acquiring language and other critical skills.

Tomasello was studying the minds of other animals to figure out what makes humans different from all the rest. To do this, he was running cognitive and behavioral tests on chimpanzees to compare their thinking and behavior with that of human infants, and his student, Brian Hare, was assisting with some of the tests.

Chimps, as our closest living relatives among the great apes, share with us a distant, unknown ancestor. But like all of the world's tree-dwelling apes, they still live in the wild much as they did millions of years ago, while our own species climbed down from the trees long ago, walked on two feet, and began taking advantage of our newly available hands in all kinds of remarkable ways.

What captivated Tomasello and came to captivate Hare was how to explain this profound difference between humans and chimpanzees. What happened to our ancestors after that first split that changed everything? Tomasello had a hunch that our unique human ability to understand the intent of other humans by following their gaze and gestures might be the answer. To test this hypothesis, he presented to the chimps in his study a series of simple assessments first used in the study of human children. He would hide a piece of food in one of two containers, and then indicate to the chimp which container held the food by simply touching, pointing to, or looking at the correct one.

The question was whether the chimps would understand the meaning communicated by these gestures, as human infants do from an early age. Some earlier test subjects, capuchin monkeys, had failed, and now it turned out that chimpanzees, our closest living genetic match, flopped just as badly, with the number of correct choices they made no better than random chance. Only chimps who had been raised by humans were able to understand what was meant by the pointing or gazing clues.

Tomasello thought this was, indeed, the answer to what set humans apart from our ape cousins. But something didn't seem quite right to Hare.

"I think my dog can do it," he blurted out one day.

His mentor laughed, but Hare persisted. His dog, Oreo, was obsessed with chasing balls, and Hare had often played a game with him in which he threw several balls in different directions and then pointed to them to show the dog where to look. Oreo had learned to stuff as many as three or four balls into his mouth at once as he followed Hare's pointing gestures, quickly snapping them up and proudly bringing them back, all crammed into his mouth like a winter's worth of nuts in the cheeks of a chipmunk. The dog had never had a minute of training to accomplish this trick.

Skeptical, Tomasello sent Hare on a mission to repeat the same tests that the chimps had failed with Oreo, who was by now getting up in years but still loved to retrieve balls as much as ever. The experiments were carried out in Hare's parents' Atlanta garage, where two food containers were presented in exactly the same way, one empty and the other full,

Brian Hare with his dog Tassie.

with Hare pointing to the correct choice. The big black dog easily selected the container with food every time.

Then Hare took his tests on the road, to some dogs he didn't know in a nearby dog daycare center, and they all passed with flying colors, too. Eventually, further trials proved to Hare and Tomasello that all dogs are able to understand the communication in human gestures from a very young age, just as human infants do. It doesn't matter whether puppies or dogs have spent time with humans or not. Somehow, through the process of coevolution, domesticated dogs have acquired an inborn ability that chimps, despite their genetic kinship to humans, have not.

Have humans, through coevolution, also learned to "speak dog"? The findings of other researchers that human volunteers can correctly identify the emotions behind dog vocalizations with a fair degree of accuracy suggests that the answer is yes, at least to some extent.

Since dogs were descended from gray wolves, the next obvious question was whether wolves, too, are born understanding human gestures. But a group of tame wolves accustomed to human contact, when tested, did no better than the chimps. Like chimps, with considerable training and socialization, the wolves proved capable of learning to follow human gestures, but unlike dogs, they did not demonstrate this skill without extensive human intervention.

The inescapable conclusion was that humans are *not* unique in this ability, after all; they share it with dogs. Somehow, during the process of domestication, dogs had evolved a basic under-standing of human communication through gaze and gesture —an understanding that no other species can match.

Since the birth of canine cognition studies in the mid-1990s, many in the field have shown that dog psychology might have important implications for the study of human development. It started the other way around, as research on human infants led cognitive psychologists, anthropologists, and evolutionary biolo-gists to consider the social skills of other animals. But it turned out that of all those animals, the dog is most like us.

This revelation led researchers around the world to begin studying dog cognition, first as a way to better understand how our own species evolved. That's still a goal for many research-ers, but now more and more dog scientists believe unraveling the mysteries of the canine mind is a worthy goal in itself, apart from the ways in which it reflects back on human beings. It's as if we've been living with an agreeable alien for thousands of years without fully understanding him. Until now. In coming to know the dog better, Hare says, we've finally begun to recognize "the genius of dogs."

How smart are they? More than a dozen research groups around the globe are currently dedicated to the study of canine thinking and behavior. Some focus on dog psychology, comparing it with that of humans and other primates, and others look at factors influencing dog-training methods, issues specific to service dogs, shelter dogs, and the human-canine bond. Most so-called dog labs explore many of these areas.

Brian Hare now runs Duke University's Canine Cognition Center (DCCC) in Durham, North Carolina, and also the university's Hominid Psychology Research Group. Comparing dog and human cognition to better understand human evolution has always been at the heart of his work, but he also sees many practical uses for discovering more about how dogs learn. So to further their knowledge of dog cognition, in 2009 the DCCC invited dog owners living near the university to volunteer their dogs to play problem-solving games in sessions ranging from a few minutes to an hour or so. It didn't take long to develop a network of one thousand dog owners willing and eager to bring their pets to the center for testing.

What's in it for the dogs? Treats and toys! But most dogs seem to love playing the games at least as much as they enjoy the rewards. According to the DCCC website, the center has "the highest acceptance rate and the cheapest tuition at Duke."

The scientifically designed games that volunteer dogs play reveal many things about how dogs learn and how they experience the world. For example, dogs seem to learn words in much the same way that human children do, by using *inferences*—logical conclusions derived from what they already know. Some dogs have larger vocabularies than others, but most are able to

Chaser, a female Border collie, has the largest tested memory of any nonhuman animal. Trained in Spartanburg, South Carolina, by her owner, the retired Wofford College professor and psychologist John Pilley, she can identify at least 1,022 toys by their names and retrieves them on command. Based on that learning, she has since moved on to further impressive feats, demonstrating her ability to understand sentences with multiple elements of grammar and to learn new behaviors by imitation.

learn the word for an unfamiliar object by putting together other cues, such as the names for objects they *do* know. If either a dog or a human toddler knows the word for the color red, for example, most will also be able to pick out the "chromium" block because it's not red—even though they have never learned that chromium is a shade of green.

One way the researchers test for dogs' ability to make inferences is to hide food in one of two places and then show the dog where the food is *not*. To find it, the dog must *infer* that if the food is not in one place, it must be in the other. In terms of comprehending language, dogs are similar to two-year-old children. They can understand as many words but are, of course, prevented from making the next leap to human speech by the limitations of their canine anatomy, if not by differences in their brains. If early humans made use of dogs as tools, it seems that dogs have also been using *humans* as tools all along. When faced with a difficult problem, a dog will quickly make eye contact with a human to enlist help—something a wolf will not do. The wolf may be better able than a dog to solve difficult problems on his own, but the dog's instinct to partner with a human has been an even more successful strategy. Social intelligence, for humans and dogs, has made all the difference.

One question being explored at DCCC is how dogs navigate their environment and form memories—do all dogs do it in the same way, or do different breeds or particular dogs within a breed have different cognitive styles? How can dogs who will make the best service dogs be identified from their individual cognitive styles, and can this knowledge help to improve training methods?

Another area of interest is trust. How do dogs form trusting relationships with humans? This understanding could help identify dogs likely to form trusting relationships with multiple handlers, with implications for both service dogs and dogs in shelters.

In early 2013, Hare helped found a project called Dognition, a web-based expansion of the testing being conducted at DCCC. The project is a way of expanding the research exponentially with the participation of dog owners around the world acting as citizen scientists. For a small fee, owners can download an application that will take them and their dogs through a series of tasks and games that assess five areas of canine intelligence: empathy, communication, cunning, memory, and reasoning. The tests come with video instructions for how to carry them out at home. For example, one simple test for empathy directs owners to yawn in the presence of their dog and observe whether the dog also yawns. If so, this indicates empathy, in the same way that human yawn copiers are said to demonstrate empathy with other humans.

Dognition users can rate their own dogs' performances, send the results to DCCC for analysis, and receive individualized reports on their dogs. The idea is to help owners better understand why their dogs behave the way they do, and at the same time provide researchers with scientific data on tens of thousands of dogs. With a greatly expanded database, researchers will be able to answer many new questions about canine cognition; with humans acting as researchers of their dogs' behavior, they often gain insights about their own behavior and learning styles as well.

At around the same time that Hare and Tomasello were discovering the unique abilities of dogs in the United States, the Hungarian ethologist and cognitive researcher Adám Miklósi had recently turned his attention from the study of an obscure east Asian fish to the equally obscure study of dog-human interactions. His advisor had suggested that such study could help explain human cognitive evolution. Miklósi and his research partner and friend József Topál weren't sure why, and they were uncertain how to even approach such a study, until a famous German child psychologist named Karin Grossman introduced them to Ainsworth's Strange Situation Test. This simple psychological test measures how children behave when a stranger enters an unfamiliar room or when their mother leaves the room. It turned out that dogs, with their human owners, behaved in the same way as young children with their mothers in these situations—a result that sent scientists in search of other behavioral parallels between dogs and humans.

The Family Dog Project, under the direction of Miklósi, is now part of the Department of Ethology at Hungary's Eötvös Loránd University in Budapest. It was established in 1994 as the first research group in the world dedicated to investigating the evolutionary and ethological foundations of the dog-human relationship. Here, too, new scientific insights are applied to practical problems through an affiliation with Dogs for Humans, which educates service dogs for the disabled. Its wide range of research projects include everything from "social learning" in dogs to dog-human attachments, wolf-dog comparisons, and how dogs specifically communicate by barking.

An early finding shows that dogs are able to learn a lot more than many people think they can, and that one of the best ways they learn is by imitation. This is really not surprising in light of coevolution, since imitation is also the main way that both

A baby boy with a European wolf pup. Humans seem to be prewired to respond to the cuteness of babies of both species, and the feeling may be mutual.

human infants and young wolves learn the skills they need to survive! Dogs can pick up fairly complex tasks simply by watching another dog or a human complete the task. Scientists first discovered that dogs are excellent at imitating their owners in 2006, when József Topál at the Hungarian Academy of Sciences in Budapest adapted "Do as I do" for teaching dogs. It was a method that had been developed in the 1950s for teaching infant chimpanzees.

Social learning, as defined by scientists at the Family Dog Project, involves one individual learning by watching a demonstrator perform some new task. Later the learner is able to perform the demonstrated task without specifically being taught to do so. It turns out that dogs are superb social learners. In a series of experiments, dogs were able to copy a human demonstrator in tasks such as detouring around a fence, opening a problem box, and operating a device that required two separate actions.

Dogs can easily be trained to "do as I do." In a series of studies, Topál worked with a trained assistance dog named Philip, who already understood and followed many commands from his disabled owner. But to test how Philip could learn new tasks, Topál began by telling the dog to stay, and then commanded, "Do as I do." The researcher then performed a simple (but unexpected and novel) action, such as jumping in place, barking, putting an object in a box, or carrying it to Philip's owner. Next, Topál spoke the cue, "Do it!" and Philip responded by matching the scientist's actions.

After this, Philip's owner realized he could teach his dog many new commands simply by demonstrating them. Soon eight more pet dogs were introduced to this method, and all proved able to learn new actions simply by observation. Not only that, but all were able to remember what they'd observed and perform it at a later time on command.

Judging by these findings, it appears that teaching dogs new tricks may be as uncomplicated as the natural teaching and learning between parent and child that goes on in families. When it comes to learning from watching humans, dogs are brilliant. At the same time, they score far behind either chimpanzees or wolves on many types of problem-solving tests. Experiments have shown that social rank—an important element of wolf pack mentality that dogs have inherited—can influence their performance in social learning tests. High-ranking (dominant) dogs were found to learn more easily by watching a human demonstrator, and low-ranking (subordinate) dogs learned better by viewing a demonstration by another dog.

The Family Dog Project has also carried out many studies of dog-human attachment. This makes sense because the most striking feature of the social life of dogs, and what sets them apart from their wolf relatives, is that they seem to prefer being with humans to being with other dogs. It's not that they don't enjoy the companionship of other dogs—they do—but given a choice, they prefer to join human social groups. As any dog owner knows, dogs look for their people when they leave and greet them joyfully when they return; they also prefer to play with their owners and play less, or not at all, when their owners are gone.

Dogs form attachments to humans that wolves, even those hand-raised by humans, never do. Their trusting relationship prompts them to turn to "their" person as a first strategy in solving a problem rather than attempting to solve it alone.

In another experiment comparing dogs, wolves, and human infants, Miklósi adapted a test devised decades before by renowned child psychologist Jean Piaget. Piaget found that if babies ten months old or younger were repeatedly shown a toy being placed in location A, they will look for the toy there even after watching it being placed in location B later on. This classic mistake has an official name: the A-not-B error. After ten months old, babies are not fooled, and cognitive scientists are still trying to figure out why younger infants make this mistake. It could be because infants are born prewired to learn from people—the same as dogs.

So Miklósi ran the A-not-B test with both dogs and wolves raised by humans. It turned out that the tame wolves would not be misled by what they'd seen humans do before; instead, they'd go straight for the correct hiding place. But dogs reacted exactly the same as nine-month-old babies, going to location A even though they'd just seen a person put the toy behind location B. Miklósi concluded that dogs, like young infants, simply choose to trust what a human has communicated, disbelieving what they've observed with their own eyes. This is social learning, whether the student is a human toddler or a dog.

How we interpret the emotional states of dogs can't help but be influenced by what we understand of human emotions. But do dogs share our human emotions? Do they feel guilty when they do something "bad"? Do they understand right and wrong? Do they have a sense of fairness and resent unequal treatment of themselves or others? These are hard questions to answer with scientific certainty, but most people who live with dogs would answer yes to all of them. That's also a perfect example of *anthropomorphism*—attributing human characteristics or motives to nonhuman animals—something we humans love to do. We even anthropomorphize forces of nature such as the weather (giving our biggest storms human names, perhaps to make them less scary), and inanimate objects (christening cars and boats with human names). So it's hard to resist similarly "humanizing" an animal as expressive as the dog. But it's also wrong, says canine cognitive expert Alexandra Horowitz, if the goal is to truly understand the dog. As she writes in her 2009 book, *Inside of a Dog: What Dogs See, Smell, and Know*, "By looking at our dogs from another perspective—from the perspective of the dog —we can see new things that don't naturally occur to those of us encumbered with human brains. So the best way to begin under-standing dogs is by forgetting what we think we know."

The first things to forget are anthropomorphisms. We see, talk about, and imagine dogs' behavior from a human-biased perspective, imposing our own emotions and thoughts on these furred creatures. Of course, we'll say, dogs love and desire; of course they dream and think; they also know and understand us, feel bored, get jealous, and become depressed. What could be a more natural explanation of a dog staring dolefully at you as you leave the house for the day than that he is depressed that you're going?

It's possible, of course, that we're guessing correctly about the emotional states of our dogs, at least some of the time. But it's just as possible that we could be completely wrong. What we need is evidence. Now dog researchers, from neuroeconomists to evolutionary biologists to cognitive scientists such as Horowitz, are beginning to provide some fascinating, sometimes surpris-ing, answers.

The results of canine cognition studies carried out to this point are as intriguing as they are provisional. Horowitz, direc-tor of the Dog Cognition Lab at Barnard College in New York City, believes that this is as it should be—that scientists should freely acknowledge how little is known about the internal lives

A wolf in a playful mood demonstrates the "play bow" that
domestic dogs have retained from their wolf origins.

187

of our familiar, beloved dogs. She loves the idea of strengthening relationships between dogs and people by getting people excited that science has only begun to investigate the secrets of the dog's mind. There is still so much to learn.

Horowitz has designed meticulous behavioral experiments to shed light on what's really going on behind irresistibly cute canine expressions that seem to speak volumes to us. Like so many dog scientists, she didn't set out to study dogs but instead was interested in comparative psychology. With a doctorate in cognitive science, she began observing dog behavior because of a deep curiosity as to which animals might possess a "theory of mind"—the understanding that others have beliefs, intents, desires, and knowledge different and apart from one's own. Normal human children usually develop this understanding no later than the age of three, though it may begin to form even earlier. When Horowitz began studying dogs, no one knew whether it developed at all in nonhuman animals. It was the early days of the current revolution in dog science. Hardly any researchers took dogs seriously as a research subject, and a universal scientific prohibition against anthropomorphism still led many to question whether dogs thought much at all or experienced emotions resembling those of humans. Few allowed that dogs might possess a theory of mind.

One reason was that experiments to confirm theory of mind were thought almost impossible to conduct with nonverbal animals because they couldn't tell you what they were thinking or feeling. Horowitz knew that in children, social play and pretending were linked to the development of a theory of mind, so she began looking at play in animals to see if this common behavior might show an understanding of others' states of mind.

Dogs, for whom play never gets old, were an obvious study subject. And sure enough, Horowitz's careful observations of canine play showed that dogs use deliberate signals to communicate and read the attitude and play readiness of other dogs.

This and other studies left little doubt that dogs have at least some rudimentary theory of mind. It also revealed to Horowitz that dogs could be an unexpectedly rewarding subject for cognitive research. And even though most of the mysteries of canine

Playful dogs with a stick . . .

. . . and a piece of rope.

cognition she and her colleagues have investigated begin with questions that almost anyone who has spent time with a dog might ask, some of the answers have been surprising.

One such question, for example, relates to the "guilty look." A trait we love in dogs is their openness and directness; we've all seen a seemingly guilty expression, if not on the faces and bodies of our own dogs, then in countless, endlessly amusing videos on the Internet. Owner comes home to find a trashcan broken into and its half-eaten contents strewn across the floor, or pillows disemboweled and fluff drifting across the couch like snow,

For human children and dogs alike, play is central to growing and learning. Most dogs, and some humans, never outgrow their sense of play.

or a favorite pair of slippers chewed and slobbered over. Dog looks guilty: head dropped, ears back, eyes averted or squinty, tail slowly, remorsefully thumping on the floor. Better yet, in a multidog household, *one* dog looks guilty, and sometimes the others even seem to point at the criminal! It's obvious who's the guilty party!

To find out if dogs really feel emotions such as guilt or remorse in these moments, volunteer dogs and owners participated in a simple test. Owners instructed their dog not to eat a treat, and then left the room. Dogs then either ate the treat or were prevented by researchers from doing so. When the owners returned, the researchers sometimes tricked them by telling them the dog had eaten the treat when he hadn't.

The result? If owners scolded them, their dogs looked guilty regardless of whether they had eaten the treat or not. The results were clear: the guilty look was associated not with what the dog did but with what the *owner* did. Dogs react to the anger of their owners by offering submissive behaviors, whether they did anything "wrong" or not. This is classic pack behavior, which young children may also exhibit—showing submission to appease the parent and head off any expected anger or punishment. And just as in human families, in multiple-dog households it may often be that the dog with the "guilty" look is simply the designated peacemaker of the family!

From the perspective of a dog, of course, stealing food is not bad behavior. It's smart strategy! But dogs are so attuned to their owners that they can often overcome this strong urge, or at least postpone it. Another researcher, Juliane Kaminski, a psychologist at the University of Portsmouth in the UK, found that dogs told by their owners not to snatch a piece of food are more likely to disobey the command in a dark room than in a well-lit room. The study dogs were four times more likely to steal the food —and steal it more quickly—when the room was dark. Not only does this show that dogs are watching their owners very, very closely, it also suggests that dogs can clearly understand that the human in the room can see things from a point of view different from their own. This is evidence that dogs do have a theory of mind—a relatively rare ability shared by great apes, elephants, dolphins, and some members of the crow family.

Like humans, dogs are great observers, but do they observe in the same way that we observe them or each other? People learn important information about one another by what psychologists call social eavesdropping. We watch how other people interact in various situations and form opinions about them that may determine how we choose to interact with those people. The question is, do dogs do the same thing as they watch the humans around them? Researchers wanted to know if dogs could distinguish between generous and selfish human food sharers by observing, without participating in, these human-human interactions.

Dogs in this study watched as a human "beggar" (one of the study participants) approached people to beg for food. The dogs observed as the generous donor gave food to the beggar, while the selfish donor refused. Some dogs saw donors just using gestures to express their generous or selfish nature, and other dogs observed donors using only their voice, and still another group of dogs saw both visual and verbal cues together. Yet another group of dogs observed a "ghost scenario," in which the donors responded in the same ways, but no human beggar was present. This was a "control" group testing whether dogs were simply reacting to the tone and gestures of donors, rather than processing the actual transactions between human beings.

Then the dogs were tested. The selfish and generous donors sat across from one another, and the dog was allowed to approach either donor. The result: dogs preferred the generous donor, spending significantly more time looking at her and interacting with her. This was most apparent in the dogs who had been exposed to the donors' vocal cues, as opposed to the gestural cues. And dogs in the ghost group showed no preference for either donor.

The researchers concluded that the dogs were definitely basing their choices on their observations of the interaction between the beggar and donors—much as humans use information from such third-party interactions. This suggests that dogs have the same capacity for complex social interactions that people have. We might even say that dogs' social skills are even *more* highly developed, since they can simultaneously respond to social cues from their own species *and* ours.

Because so much of canine intelligence is based on the sensory input of odors, canine cognitive scientists have been especially interested in learning more about how dogs navigate the world using their noses. The canine sense of smell has not diminished with domestication, and it is one of the most striking examples of coevolution between dogs and humans. In a very real and measurable way, dogs and humans evolved complementary abilities, joined forces, and together became more successful in the world than either had been alone. With dogs, we no longer needed to depend on our noses for survival so much because we could depend on *theirs*. Gaining the help of their acute sense of hearing was another huge plus. And by partnering with us, dogs got the immense benefit of tool-making hands and problem-solving abilities far beyond those of their wolf cousins.

Here are the relevant stats: A dog's brain is roughly one-tenth the size of a human's. The prefrontal cortex, which governs problem-solving and decision-making, makes up 30 percent of the human brain but only 7 percent of the dog brain. The olfactory cortex, which processes scent information, accounts for 12.5 percent of the dog's total brain mass, but less than 1 percent of the human's brain.

Many studies suggest that wild canids can outperform domestic dogs in *nonsocial* problem-solving experiments, indicating that domestic dogs may have lost much of their original problem-solving abilities once they joined humans, but gained new problem-solving strategies by that very partnership. Interestingly, humans' sense of smell, compared with that of other primates, has also declined during the course of our evolution. It's clear that complimentary smelling abilities were absolutely vital to the unique partnership between humans and dogs from the very beginning.

Particular breeds of dogs have long been trained to use that inborn ability for many useful activities, including tracking missing persons and detecting everything from drugs to diseases, impending seizures and hidden explosives. But what about ordinary, untrained dogs? Is it only specially developed and trained bloodhounds or German shepherds who can accomplish such

Morgan, a detection dog in training at the Penn Vet Working Dog Center, practices the "scent wall." He smells each of the "ports" to find where drugs are hidden. Morgan graduated with high marks, and is currently a narcotics detection dog with the New Jersey State Police.

tasks, or could most dogs, under the right circumstances, do nearly as well? Researchers at the Dog Cognition Lab wanted to know.

In one study they began testing how well untrained pet dogs can detect quantity by using just their noses. Previous research had shown that dogs can visually discriminate between greater or lesser quantities of food; this test of sixty-four dogs showed that they do not reliably distinguish between quantities when the food can be smelled but not seen. When given a choice between closed plates holding either one or five morsels of food, the difference in preference was not significant, although the dogs did spend more time investigating the plates with more food. Another finding was that if the owners showed more interest in a plate holding less food, their dogs were more likely to approach that plate than the one holding more. Adding a strong, unexpected odor to a visibly larger food quantity, on the other hand, caused dogs to reject that larger quantity in favor of a smaller amount without the foreign odor. This study did show that although some dogs can be trained to use their olfactory abilities in highly specialized ways that the average pet dog would not be able to do, all dogs are born with sophisticated olfactory equipment that helps them read their world through scent that puts our puny human smelling sense to shame.

A WORLD OF SMELLS

Imagine how it would be if every detail of your visual world was matched by a corresponding smell. Imagine smelling every minute of the day and night in visual detail—receiving a constant stream of detailed information from sources far outside your ability to see them with your eyes. This is the experience of the average dog, whose nose is tens of thousands of times more sensitive to odors than our own.

Humans are profoundly visual creatures. We have excellent vision, and we rely on it above all other senses to navigate our world. Not so our hearing abilities, which are inferior to most other mammals'. We compensate somewhat for this lack by having brains that are exceptionally good at distinguishing between very similar sounds, a skill we evolved to decode speech.

A dog's vision isn't bad; it's roughly comparable to our own except for minor deficits in color perception, which are more than offset by their superior night vision. Their hearing is much more sensitive than ours—about four times better within their optimal range. This range includes everything that we can hear, plus much that we can't hear at all—the higher frequency we call ultrasound, but which, to a dog, is simply sound.

But a dog's eyes, and even his sensitive ears, are just backup; in a study in which police tracker dogs were provided a scent trail that seemed to run in the opposite direction to a set of footprints, they followed their noses and ignored the footprints every time. Amazingly, trained tracking dogs can disregard the barrage of odors entering their noses, as well as visual and auditory distractions, to focus on the one specific scent they've been asked to detect.

Each dog's nose is unique, like a human fingerprint. If every dog were nose-printed, we could identify each one in a canine nasal database. And the olfactory part of a dog's brain is forty times larger than a human's; depending on the breed, a dog can have up to 300 million olfactory receptors in his nose, compared to about 6 million in ours. Even with that extreme superiority in equipment, dogs don't merely smell a superstrong version of what we smell (or don't smell); instead, they can perceive multiple *layers* of smell, which gives dogs a far greater range of information.

Dogs' noses also function quite differently from ours. When we humans inhale, we smell and breathe through the same airways within our noses. But when dogs inhale, a fold of tissue just inside their nostrils helps to split these two functions. One directs airflow to the olfactory receptors in the back of the nose, and the other moves air into the lungs. The olfactory area of a dog's nose filters odor-laden air through a labyrinth of bony, scroll-like structures called turbinates, where odor molecules are sorted out based on their individual chemical properties.

Dogs receive important information when they *exhale,* as well as when they inhale. When we exhale, we send the old air out of our noses in the same way it came in, forcing out any incoming odors at the same time. But when dogs exhale, the spent air exits through special slits in the sides of their noses. This helps usher new odors into the dog's nose, allowing him to sniff more or less continuously.

Dogs also have a *second* olfactory system, a separate structure located in the bottom of the nasal passage called the vomeronasal organ.

A dog's nose, wonder of nature.

It's dedicated to detecting chemicals called pheromones—hormonelike substances that communicate specific information from one species to another, often having to do with reproductive status and social behavior. Many other animals have a vomeronasal organ, but so far there's no conclusive evidence that humans do.

A dog can wiggle each nostril independently. Try it! We humans can't. Nor can we tell into which nostril an odor has arrived, as dogs can. This helps them to locate the source of a smell. And we all know that healthy dogs have wet noses, but why? Having a moist nose helps dogs to better pick up scents—a thin layer of mucus on the nose boosts the detection of scents, and dogs can also lick their noses to sample the scent by mouth.

In the world of dogs, every object, and every part of every object, has its own scent and conveys different types of information. Not only can traces of scent tell a dog who or what has touched a flower or a lamppost, they can also give the dog a pretty good idea of when this happened. In this way, by perceiving the character and strength of urine left by another dog, for example, a dog may understand something of the passage of time. The "age" of the scent mark is a guide to how long ago the dog who left the scent passed that location, as well as many other details about that dog. The dog's nose is so sensitive, it may even be able to detect subtle differences from one footstep to the next as he follows a human's scent trail. Maybe that same powerful nose can also imagine the future, in a way, by picking up odors that reveal that another dog or animal may soon be approaching.

Dogs have been known to successfully follow a scent trail that's more than a week old, find a body submerged in water more than eighty feet deep, and locate a plastic container packed with thirty-five pounds of marijuana submerged in gasoline within a gas tank. They can detect some odors in parts per trillion. What does this mean? Alexandra Horowitz explains it in this way: a human's sense of smell might detect whether a teaspoon of sugar has been added to a cup of coffee, but a dog can detect that teaspoon of sugar in one million gallons of water—enough to fill two Olympic-size pools. Dogs can smell chemical odors caused by diseases such as cancer in humans, often before any medical test can find them. They can tell what we've eaten, where we've been, whom we've met, and what we've done, and yes, they can also smell our emotions. Fear, for example, causes humans and other animals to emit certain pheromones. If a dog can't tell we're afraid or anxious by our body language, which he can, he will surely know it by our odor.

We have language, and dogs, as far as we can tell, do not. We have *so* many words for colors, patterns, textures, sizes, and shapes, and relatively few for smells. If your dog had words, and opposable thumbs to operate a keyboard or pen, he might write a multivolume dictionary dedicated to the names and descriptions of smells alone. It would make for fascinating reading.

7

A WOLF ON THE BED

We've come a long way with our dogs since that distant day when a young boy and his wolf-dog entered the darkness of a limestone cave perched on the side of a cliff in southern France, and together they perused an already-ancient gallery of painted beasts. The world we inhabit today would be unrecognizable to that boy, but he would probably understand our dogs, even if most of them bear little resemblance to his own.

Good catch!

The basic reasons dogs have traveled with us through time are the same as ever. More than any other animal in the world, dogs freely offer us companionship and protection, expertly perform specialized jobs to help us live better, and happily go wherever we want to go. They're playmates who never tire of our games and the most sympathetic listeners when we need to talk. They hang on our every word, their intelligent eyes gazing deeply into our own, but they never talk back. In return, the most fortunate dogs are provided for as lovingly as if they were our children. They're no longer obliged to hunt for survival, but instead they're offered new ways to use their innate hunting ability to do *our* work. When we work, they may work alongside us, and when we rest, they rest with us—often curled up on our beds—but always with an ear cocked, ready to warn us of danger.

Many people consider their dogs full-fledged family members. New scientific evidence reveals sound biological and evolutionary reasons for this feeling. As Japanese researchers reported in the journal *Science,* when dogs and their owners gaze into one another's eyes, both experience a surge of oxytocin, a powerful hormone that promotes love and attachment in mammals. It's this hormone that acts to bind parents and children.

In a study involving thirty dog owners and their pets,

Like wolves, dogs form strong social bonds with other dogs. But unlike wolves, they often form even stronger bonds with humans.

researchers found that the longer dogs and humans locked eyes, the more oxytocin was released. But when the same study was conducted with human-raised wolves and the people who had raised them, the results were very different. The wolves barely looked at the humans—most likely because wolves generally consider eye contact an aggressive challenge or a way of sizing up a competitor. Not surprisingly, oxytocin levels failed to go up for either the wolves or their handlers in this study.

The researchers concluded that this unique hormonal feedback mechanism was probably absent in the wolf ancestors of dogs, only appearing at some later point in their evolutionary history. Perhaps the now-extinct subset of wolves who became the first dogs had it, too. We will probably never know.

The study was the first to show oxytocin at work in two members of different species, another strong indicator of coevolution, said the scientists. Not only have dogs adopted this fundamental

The love of a boy and his dog, cemented with the help of oxytocin.

human bonding chemistry, but it's also likely that humans had to change, too, evolving the ability to bond in this unique way with another species. The rush of oxytocin generated by mutual human-dog gazing prompts longer gazing, which produces even greater oxytocin levels, fueling a positive feedback loop not unlike that between a mother and child. According to Emory University neuroscientist Larry Young, who was not involved in this study, the results suggest that over the course of domestication, there was strong selective pressure favoring dogs able to bond with a human caretaker in this way.

"Evolution took the easy route," he said, "and used the neural mechanisms already in place to create mother-infant bonds, tweaked them slightly, perhaps through neoteny, or preservation of infant-like traits [in dogs] into adulthood."

The shared oxytocin feedback loop is one good reason dogs quite naturally gravitate toward humans, often seeming to understand how to live and work in human company without being taught how to do it. It's almost as if dogs are born to live with us.

It's also true that the vast majority of dogs in the world still live on the fringes of human society, rather than in the embrace of loving families. In some parts of the world, no one spends much money on large numbers of "street dogs," most of whom look similar and live precarious lives of little affection or care but infinite freedom. But even under those circumstances, dogs survive and even thrive. Their appearance and behavior vary according to the conditions of the places they inhabit, rather than the preferences of people. Centuries of humans' selective breeding of dogs have produced physical and behavioral traits unknown to wild wolves, and many of these traits now help stray dogs survive and breed among, near, but not housed with humans.

A fascinating example of what happens to dogs when humans aren't directly involved in their care is the feral dog population of Moscow, Russia's capital city. Some thirty-five thousand homeless dogs live within the city limits and have done so for at least 150 years. Most are not lost pets, but dogs born homeless who have sometimes banded together for survival. Over the years Moscow's street dogs have lost traits such as spotted coloration, wagging tails, and friendliness toward humans that distinguish domesticated dogs from wolves—but they haven't *become* wolves. Most are medium-size, with thick fur, wedge-shaped heads, almond eyes, long tails, and semi-erect ears.

Survival is difficult for a stray, and estimates are that no more than about 3 percent of them ever breed. Those who do survive are the toughest and the cleverest. The pressures under which they live have led them to separate into four distinct behavioral types, referred to by Muscovites as the guard dogs (those who follow security personnel around and treat these humans as the alpha leaders of their packs), the scavengers (shy dogs who roam the city for garbage rather than interacting with people), the wild dogs (the most wolflike dogs, feral and nocturnal, who

A stray dog rests in a pool of sunlight at a Moscow metro station on a frigid day. The train station provides some shelter from outside temperatures, which dropped that week in January 2010 to -13 degrees Fahrenheit (-25 Celsius).

avoid humans, view them as a threat, and live in the woods on the outskirts of the city and eat whatever they can catch), and the last, most amazing group, the beggars.

The beggars are highly intelligent and socialized to people, but not affectionate or personally attached to them. The alpha dog among them isn't the best hunter or the strongest, but the smartest. One street-savvy subgroup of beggars, called the metro dogs, behaves much like human commuters. They travel about the city using the extensive public transportation system, relying on handouts of food from human commuters. To succeed at this strategy, the dogs have learned to navigate the subway on their own. They seem to know stops by name and will integrate a number of specific stations into their territories. They ride the train cars confidently, often in a businesslike manner, and most of their fellow (human) commuters treat them with tolerance, if not outright affection. Many people regularly feed the dogs and even build makeshift shelters for them during the harsh Moscow winters.

Metro dogs are rarely hit by cars; they've learned to cross the streets when people do, and many are seen waiting to cross when no pedestrians are around—suggesting that they've learned to recognize the green "walking man" image on the crosswalk traffic signal. Packs of metro dogs seldom fight each other, but they vigilantly guard the city against the wild dogs and wolves living on the outskirts. Their remarkable intelligence and adaptive skills have led some longtime observers to wonder if the strong selection for intellect may transform Moscow's metro dogs into an entirely separate species in time if humans don't intervene in their welfare.

Judging from the dramatic differences between a Chihuahua and a Great Dane, domestic dogs in general already may be on their way to becoming a separate species, at least according to the accepted definition of interbreeding capability.

How much time might it take for dogs to fully separate from wolves and become their own species? And what parts of the genome will determine how that happens, *if* it happens? What selective pressures would cause such a shift? The remarkably adaptable, changeable dog will answer those questions as we continue to evolve together into the future.

Moscow's feral dogs live in a delicate balance alongside the human population, but in other cities the situation is quite

This Great Dane and Chihuahua show the extreme diversity in the size and shape of skulls (and other body parts) of domestic dogs today. Early dogs in the Paleolithic had not yet developed such extremes, and, according to current scientific thinking, more closely resembled the now-extinct wolf populations from which they descended.

different. For example, animal control officials in San Francisco have approached their city's homeless dog situation with a creative solution—the first of its kind in the country—assigning dogs needing foster care to homeless individuals in exchange for the person's agreement to give up panhandling. Carefully screened volunteer foster "parents," in return, receive help in securing stable housing and a small stipend for providing care and socialization to homeless dogs and puppies until they're ready for adoption.

Yet in some Asian cultures, street dogs are considered food, sold in markets like chickens. There is no universal way of being with dogs, but everywhere in the world, people live in *some* way with dogs.

SEATTLE DOG MASTERS PUBLIC TRANSIT

Eclipse, a young female black Labrador mix, became an instant Internet celebrity in January 2015, when she demonstrated that dogs don't have to be feral to figure out how to get around on their own in a big city. Eclipse is the well-loved companion of Jeff Young, who lives very close to a bus stop and regularly takes his dog on the bus to visit a nearby dog park. One day, when Young wasn't quite ready to get on the bus when it pulled up to the stop, Eclipse took matters into her own paws and hopped up the steps into the bus alone. She found a seat by a window and watched for her stop, then waited for the driver to open the door and hopped out. So Young, unconcerned, took the next bus and caught up with her at the dog park. A few days later, Eclipse repeated her solo ride, and it became something of a routine.

Young explained that Eclipse, after living in the city with him for two years, is "urbanized. She's a bus-riding, sidewalk-walking dog."

All the city bus drivers and many fellow passengers know Eclipse. One fellow commuter explained, "She sits here just like a person does. She makes everybody happy." A Metro Transit spokesperson said the company is happy that a dog can appreciate public transit, though technically Eclipse should be on a leash. But leash or no leash, she knows where she's going, and she's a dog in a hurry.

Family companions, surrogate children, wily street beggars: dogs are all of these today. But many also have careers. Dogs have always had jobs, from the earliest days when wolves joined their superb hunting skills with those of our prehistoric ancestors. Since then, most of the work of dogs has been based on their exquisite sense of smell—the whole basis of detection work, as well as the basis of human hunting with dogs. It's just that for some twenty-first-century dogs, the "prey" is now a hidden stash of illicit drugs, a ticking bomb, or a child wandering, lost, in the wilderness. Some dogs have even been trained to sniff out bed bugs in city apartments.

For thousands of years, dogs have willingly lent untold "dog hours" to humans, doing jobs for which they were uniquely suited. For what is a dog without a job? In a wolf pack, each individual has a job to do, and dogs, sharing more than 99 percent of their DNA with wolves, still thrive on knowing their jobs and performing them well. Those jobs have changed, but because of their abiding trust in humans, most dogs happily embrace any task their humans set for them, from patrolling the front lines of a war zone to becoming the eyes or ears of people with disabilities to comforting the sick and the lonely and providing a nonjudgmental ear to children practicing newfound reading skills.

THE DOGS OF 9/11

Bretagne, a gentle golden retriever, was only a pup, barely two, when she and her handler, Denise Corliss, arrived from Texas at the site of the fallen World Trade Center in Lower Manhattan, New York City. All told, at least four hundred specially trained dogs were deployed, with their human partners, in the immediate aftermath of a coordinated series of four terrorist attacks using hijacked commercial airliners as weapons on that bright fall day in 2001. Eventually, the appalling death toll of nearly three thousand would become known, but in the immediate aftermath of the plane crashes, legions of volunteer human and canine first responders were deployed to look for victims and survivors at two of the three attack sites in New York City and Washington, D.C. Bretagne was the youngest dog.

She worked exhausting twelve-hour days alongside about three hundred other dogs, searching for survivors. After it became clear that no survivors would be found in the smoking rubble of the towers, a second group of dogs specially trained to find human remains was brought in. Therapy dogs came, too, to help human first responders at the scene cope with the magnitude of the tragedy.

But as it turned out, *all* of the dogs provided therapy, whether specifically trained for that job or not, just by doing what dogs do best. Spending a few quiet moments with one of these dogs, touching them and receiving sloppy kisses in return, brought comfort and solace to traumatized rescue workers. The dogs made it possible for human responders to keep going through the devastating search, and the dogs ultimately found many of the human remains, bringing needed closure to the families of victims.

Many of the dogs went on to use their highly refined detection skills in other disasters and emergencies. Bretagne helped in rescue efforts after Hurricanes Katrina, Rita, and Ivan. In her later years the veteran rescue dog, her soft coat now turned nearly white, worked happily as a therapy dog in Texas elementary schools, helping special needs children learn to read by listening intently and nonjudgmentally as they hesitantly sounded out the words of their books to her.

Other 9/11 dogs retired to enjoy many more healthy years as companions to their handlers. Few, if any, appeared to have suffered any long-term effects from their exposure to toxic dust and other hazards in the days following 9/11—in striking contrast to human first responders who worked alongside these dogs through those long days and nights, a number of whom have since developed serious ailments such as cancers and lung disorders.

To try to understand why these dogs have fared so much better than some of the human volunteers, and to help predict the possible health effects on humans from exposure, Dr. Cynthia Otto has spent years conducting a long-term study monitoring the lifelong health of all the dogs who served at Ground Zero. She's a critical care veterinarian and a professor at the University of Pennsylvania's veterinary hospital and School of Veterinary Medicine She was at Ground Zero in the days after the towers fell as part of the Pennsylvania search-and-rescue team working under the Federal Emergency Management Agency. She concluded that a combination of physical and anatomical differences between dogs and humans may explain the dogs' surprising resilience under those conditions. Identifying these differences will help researchers understand how to help both human and dog responders to future disasters.

On September 11, 2012, the Penn Vet Working Dog Center opened under Otto's direction, with its first enrolled class of seven puppies in training, all named after original 9/11 dogs: Bretagne, Kaiserin, Morgan, Papa Bear, Sirius, Socks, and Thunder. At the time they were seven bundles of floppy, goofy, energetic puppyness in whom it was sometimes difficult to detect future greatness. But by the time they'd completed their training, these dogs, and those who followed them, were some of the best-prepared detection dogs in the world.

The original Bretagne and her young namesake meet at the opening ceremony of the Penn Vet Working Dog Center, eleven years after the first Bretagne deployed to Ground Zero in New York City in the aftermath of a terrorist attack on the World Trade Center Twin Towers.

Quest, training for a career as a police dog at the Penn Vet Working Dog Center when he was a puppy. Here he's practicing agility and environmental exposure. Nowadays he's a patrol and explosive-detection dog for the Southeastern Pennsylvania Transportation Authority (SEPTA).

Parsons, a young search-and-rescue dog in training, working on a practice rubble pile. He seems to have found what he was searching for, and he's not letting go!

In addition to developing some dogs' remarkable abilities at detection, scientists are finding many more ways in which dogs can enhance human health and well-being. Just by being dogs, they provide important health benefits — not only for individual humans' health, but also for the advancement of medical science, which helps large numbers of both dogs and humans.

Some of the most cutting-edge research in the biological sciences is focused on what's known as the microbiome — the total "community" of microbes (bacteria, viruses, and parasites), each with its associated genome. Scientists have identified the microbiome as a startlingly significant part of living organisms, including both humans and dogs. According to current estimates, every human body harbors over ten times more microbial cells than human cells; dogs' bodies likely harbor equally large percentages. While it's long been known that some microbes cause diseases, in the last few years scientists have recognized that our bodies are also home to beneficial microbes that are crucial in maintaining health. Beneficial bacteria colonize the gut, skin, and urogenital tract at birth, creating complex microbial communities that develop and evolve, just as the host organism does, living and changing in a symbiotic relationship that is thought to affect health and disease, reproduction, mate choice, and ultimately, perhaps, even evolution itself.

A new "hologenomic theory of evolution" (as yet unproven,

but supported by some early research) proposes that the forces of natural selection that Darwin described act not only on the totality of the individual, but also on its associated microbiome. Since microorganisms are transmitted from one generation to the next, and since microbial communities can change rapidly in response to environmental stresses, scientists who subscribe to this theory believe microbial genes may play a crucial role in the adaptation and evolution of many higher organisms.

The implications of this idea are profound. If the microbes in our bodies can cause and prevent diseases, affect our mental states and our choices of mating partners—and even, as at least one study has suggested, make possible the development of new species—then our scientific understanding of evolution will have taken a huge and unexpected turn.

If any of us doubts whether our long evolutionary path with dogs is a thing of the past, research into the microbiome seems poised to set those doubts to rest. Dog owners, it turns out, share a common bacterial mix on their skins—a particular microbial salad that scientists have identified. This is true even of dog owners who have never met; it's as if there's a generic "dog bacteria" mixture that most pet dogs share. Carried into our houses on the paws, noses, and tongues of pet dogs, these invisible life forms then colonize the skin of humans through close contact such as petting and kissing. It's probably good that we can't see them, and most of us don't give these invisible "colonists" a thought when interacting with our dogs. But scientists are only now beginning to appreciate how these microscopic populations play a critical role in keeping people healthy, in part by helping immune systems and metabolisms to function properly. Even though modern medical knowledge and hygienic practices have succeeded in protecting people from exposure to *harmful* bacteria to the point where some of the beneficial bugs are also kept at bay, families who live with dogs get a healthful dose without even trying. Surprisingly, studies have shown that married couples share more microorganisms with their dog than with each other!

Beneficial bacteria on people's skin and in their gastrointestinal tracts help to prevent inflammation and control disease-causing bacteria. Many scientists now suspect that gut bacteria also play a key role in mood disorders and a range of other mental illnesses. There is still much to be learned about this gut-brain connection, but neuroscientists feel certain that the immune system plays a big part, as does the vagus nerve, which connects the human brain to the digestive tract. Scientists have shown that some

Sloppy dog kisses, we now know, have medicinal properties.

types of intestinal bacteria produce important neurotransmitters that affect the brain, influencing everything from anxiety to depression to autism and other mental illnesses.

So it's not surprising that people who live with dogs enjoy a long list of proven health advantages, whether they know it or not. Children who grow up in households with dogs have lower rates of asthma and eczema, and their immune systems function better than those without dogs in the home.

But beneficial dog germs are just the beginning. Adults who share their lives with dogs enjoy better cardiovascular health, lower blood pressure and cholesterol, more resistance to stress, and improved fitness than their dogless counterparts. These benefits accrue at least in part because dog owners tend to exercise more regularly, spend more time outdoors, and interact with a wider range of other people and dogs. Enhanced social interaction is known to improve health, well-being, and longevity. And caring for a canine companion can give both children and adults a greater sense of purpose. Sometimes, especially for people who are elderly or socially isolated, a dog really *is* a best friend—the primary social relationship in their lives.

Dogs are more important than ever before in understanding human health, in part because of what medical researchers can learn by studying diseases shared by both species—new understandings that are already benefiting both humans and dogs. This convergence has spawned a medical movement called One Health, a collaboration between medical and veterinary doctors, who join forces to better understand and treat the shared diseases of humans and other animals—especially dogs. For example, about six million dogs are diagnosed with cancer every year—frequently the same types of cancers that afflict humans. This is both unfortunate for the dogs and beneficial for our human understanding of these diseases. It's now possible for researchers to isolate genes associated with various cancers and to look at the interactions between genetics and the environment in a whole range of cancers that affect both humans and dogs.

A similar cross-species convergence is seen in the elderly. Old dogs sometimes get Alzheimer's disease, just as older people may, but with their shorter life spans, the course of the disease takes a lot fewer years than it does in humans, making it easier for researchers to search for ways to slow or prevent age-related dementias. Respiratory diseases and diabetes are among many other diseases the two species share, along with an inherited disease of the retina—macular degeneration—that eventually leads to blindness. Clinical trials for these diseases are often easier to run on dogs, providing doctors animal models of human diseases, and at the same time increasing the chances for curing canines.

Dogs are also playing a more active role in human health, using the awesome power of their noses to make diagnoses that sometimes defy modern medicine. Medical detection dogs are the canine diagnosticians of modern health care. Cancer-sniffing dogs can detect various types of human cancers—with up to 99 percent accuracy—often long before standard tests reveal any abnormality at all. So far, dogs have been trained to identify tumors of the lung, breast, skin, bladder, ovaries, and prostate, providing a diagnosis just by using their noses, without invasive and expensive procedures. They can detect the faintest of scents given off by cancers in tissue samples, urine, and even in a patient's breath. Researchers hope eventually to develop an "electronic nose" that mimics a dog's ability to smell diseases, but for now, real dogs are proving that low-tech solutions can lead the way to technological breakthroughs.

If medical detection canines are researchers, medical assistance dogs are the daily caretakers who guard the health and well-being of people with disabilities and chronic diseases. The same ability to identify tumors by smell gives dogs a talent for sniffing out subtle changes in body chemistry caused by chronic diseases. This inborn skill can be lifesaving when highly trained medical assistance dogs are paired with people who have diabetes, for example. These dogs' job is to help detect spiking and plummeting blood sugar levels that can be dangerous or even fatal if not quickly corrected. They're trained to recognize the scent of sugar fluctuations before symptoms are felt so people take corrective, potentially life-saving measures.

Other assistance dogs can predict when someone will have an epileptic seizure as long as forty-five minutes before it occurs, giving the person time to prepare or even, potentially, to avert the episode. No one knows for sure how the dogs do this.

Dogs can also be eyes for the blind and ears for the deaf. They can find lost children, fetch items for people with disabilities, and comfort those who suffer from post-traumatic stress disorder. They can open and close drawers, doors, and refrigerators. Some have even been trained to answer the phone and respond to knocks on the door, and they can serve as fire alarms. Everyone has heard stories of dogs saving their sleeping families by alerting them to housefires. For this lifesaving feat, dogs need no special training, but a loud, insistent bark definitely helps!

The ability of trained assistance dogs to calm agitation in and smooth social interactions for autistic children may be linked, in part, to the beneficial bacteria dogs often share with these children, but microbes are probably not the whole story. Just spending time with a special dog often improves language skills, social interactions, and the ability to perceive and express emotions. It can also help autistic children develop greater confidence in touching others and in being touched.

Some might suggest that these are the same cognitive and emotional benefits that *all* people who include dogs in their lives enjoy. They are among the very same benefits that ancient humans must have discovered when they invited some unusually social wolves into their camps and began to evolve a level

A search-and-rescue dog digs through the snow. A S&R dog can sometimes find avalanche victims buried in deep snow in time to save their lives.

of social intelligence, language, and culture unknown in any of their primate relatives to this day.

At the same time, social scientists are zeroing in on the ways the ancient human-canine bond is enhancing the health not only of individuals, but of whole communities. For example, a 2007 Australian study based on qualitative data obtained through focus groups at suburban community centers found that pet dogs in a community act as facilitators of social contact, interaction, and trust among neighborhood residents. The researchers also found that the human-canine bond improved the health, fitness, and psychological well-being of individuals and entire communities. It's not hard to imagine our ancient ancestors benefiting in the same ways when they began hunting cooperatively with the wolves who became dogs and formed hybrid human-canine packs. It may even be the secret of our evolutionary success.

Despite years of intensive study—ever since Charles Darwin, in 1868, raised the question of whether dogs had evolved from a single species or a mix of several wild canids—dog researchers still can't agree on where and when wolves became humans' loyal companions. Today dog domestication is one of the most competitive and contentious areas of evolutionary biology, as international teams of geneticists and paleontologists publish competing theories and countertheories. As the first and arguably the most fully domesticated species, dogs could hold the key to human prehistory and to the very nature of domestication itself.

Now a new spirit of international cooperation is promising to finally settle the question of when and where wolves first gave rise to early dogs. For the first time, formerly warring researchers are sharing samples and data from the analysis of thousands of ancient canid bones. By combining information from ancient DNA with a relatively new technique known as geometric morphometrics, which involves taking thousands of measurements of bones to see how their shapes differ among individuals and subjecting them to computer analysis, researchers are beginning to get a much clearer picture of the world's first domesticated species. Major findings are beginning to take shape.

Large dogs have been used to carry items for humans since Paleolithic times. This is a historic photo, published between 1900 and 1930. A handwritten caption reveals that the dog was named Prince and he carried utensils on his back in Seward, Alaska.

Most researchers now agree that the first stage of dog domestication could have begun with wolves who dared to come close enough to discarded animal carcasses that human hunter-gatherers left on the outskirts of their campsites, though some remain convinced that the process began with humans deliberately taking very young wolf pups into their families and raising them with their own children. In either case, those tamer, bolder wolves survived longer and produced more pups, who produced even bolder pups over succeeding generations. Sooner or later the offspring of one of those pups dared to come close enough to eat out of a human hand. Then, once our ancestors realized how useful these friendly wolves could be, a second phase of more human-directed domestication began, with the deliberate breeding of early dogs to become even better hunters, herders, and guardians.

In some ancient dog and wolf skeletons, researchers have observed a flattening of particular vertebrae in the spine, suggesting that these animals may have hauled heavy packs on their backs. In others, they noticed missing pairs of molars near the rear of the jaws, indicating that these animals may have worn some sort of bridle to pull carts or sleds. Besides their obvious use in hunting, these additional jobs may have been critical for human survival and the ability to transition from a hunter-gatherer existence to a more settled life based on farming. As cooperating teams of scientists continue to analyze thousands of wolf, dog, and still unclassified specimens, major breakthroughs in the understanding of dog domestication seem just around the corner.

If they didn't walk on all fours, lack opposable thumbs, and communicate with limited vocabularies of barks, whines, growls, and meaningful gazes—like thought bubbles suspended over their heads—we might start to imagine that dogs are simply furry human beings, after all. Many dog owners *do,* in fact, admit to viewing their pets as their children. So it's not surprising that dogs in our culture are increasingly seen as deserving of their own identity as "persons," including legal protections and basic civil rights. Dog ownership, more and more, is seen as dog "parenting." This is no small change, since parenting implies responsibility and concern for another's well-being, which ownership does not. Dog law is now a rising specialty in the legal field, as courts are asked to settle complicated and emotional questions of custody, inheritance, and liability involving dogs that would have been thought frivolous just a few years ago.

This is a major shift in how we view both dogs and ourselves —as partners, companions, and family members who are more alike than different, more equal than not. We might say it's a shift *back*—to the long-ago time when a subset of hunting-and-gathering primates joined forces with some of their top competitors instead of looking upon them as prey.

For many people today, dogs are essential—a bridge between the human world of walls and wires and abstract concepts and the wild, animal world—a natural world of sights, sounds, and smells, and the distant memory of our own evolutionary past. In our dogs' eyes we see reflected who we are and from where we've come.

Wolves and dogs, despite common origins and shared genetic profiles, are distinctly different animals. One is wild and always will be; the other lives fully in human culture —firmly linked with us—and always has. In this, the dog is truly unique: our best friend and partner through time.

GLOSSARY

anthropology: the science of human beings, especially of their physical characteristics, their origins, their environment and social relations, and their culture

canid: any of a family *(Canidae)* of carnivorous animals that includes the wolves, jackals, foxes, coyotes, and domestic dogs

coevolution: the influence of closely associated species on each other in their evolution

cognition: conscious mental activities—thinking, understanding, learning, and remembering

convergence: the independent development of similar characteristics (such as the bodily structure or cultural traits of unrelated organisms) often associated with similarity of habits or environment

DNA: genetic material that carries all the information about how a living organism will look and function

domestication: the breeding or training of an animal to need and accept the care of human beings; growing a plant for human use

ethology: the scientific and objective study of animal behavior especially under natural conditions

evolution: the process by which changes in plants and animals happen over time

evolutionary biology: the branches of biology that deal with the processes of change in populations of organisms, especially taxonomy, paleontology, ethology, population genetics, and ecology

genetics: a branch of biology that focuses on the heredity and variation of organisms

genome: the total genetic material of an organism

hologenomic evolution: an emerging evolutionary theory that proposes that an object of natural selection is not just the individual organism, but rather the organism together with its associated microbial communities

Ice Age: the series of glacial episodes during the Pleistocene period

molecular biology: a field of science concerned with the chemical structures and processes of biological phenomena at the molecular level

mutation: a change in the genes of a plant or animal that creates physical characteristics that are different from what is considered normal

neurotransmitter: a substance in the body that carries a signal from one nerve cell to another

paleoanthropology: a branch of anthropology focusing on fossil hominids

Paleolithic: relating to the time during the early Stone Age when people made rough tools and weapons out of stone, beginning about 2.5 to 2 million years ago, and ending about 10,000 years ago in Europe and the Middle East

radiocarbon dating: the determination of the age of objects of organic origin by measuring the radioactivity of their carbon content

Notes

1. Close Encounters of the Canine Kind

4 "Chimpanzees are individualists. They are boisterous": Wolfgang M. Schleidt and Michael D. Shatler, "Co-Evolution of Humans and Canids: An Alternative View of Dog Domestication," *Evolution and Cognition* 9, no. 1 (2003): 60. Though now somewhat out of date, this is interesting as one of the first published papers to suggest and explore the concept of coevolution between dogs and humans.

17 "The oldest evidence of domesticated dogs": Ker Than, "Oldest Domesticated Dog in Americas Found—Was Human Food," *National Geographic News*, January 19, 2011, news .nationalgeographic.com/news/2011/01/110118-oldest-domestic -dogs-north-america-eaten-texas-cave-science-animals.

2. Written in the Bones

29 "You care for nothing but shooting, dogs and rat-catching": Darwin recounts this exchange with his father in his autobiography, *The Life and Letters of Charles Darwin* (New York: D. Appleton and Co., 1897), edited by his son Francis Darwin and published five years after Darwin's death. The book is based on Charles Darwin's extensive personal and professional correspondence.

30 "If it could be shown": Charles Darwin, *The Variation of Animals and Plants under Domestication* [1868] (Baltimore: Johns Hopkins University Press, 1998).

32 "The strongest and most active animal": Erasmus Darwin, *Zoonomia* [1794] (Middlesex, UK: Echo Library, 2007).
"No doubt a single, original race": Jean-Baptiste Lamarck, *Philosophie Zoologique (Zoological Philosophy)* [1809] (Chicago: Univ. of Chicago Press, 1984). For more information, see www .pbs.org/wgbh/evolution/library/02/3_023_02.html.

3. Wolf-Dogs: Those Skulls Are *How* Old?

54 "the kindest dog ever": Mietje Germonpré, in personal email correspondence with the author, May 26, 2014.

56 "When I received the results of the date": Ibid.

68 "It's the differences in the words of": James Gorman, "'What Is' Meets 'What If': The Role of Speculation in Science," *New York Times*, May 24, 2012.

4. A Meeting of Minds

87 "In a series of forms graduating insensibly": Charles Darwin, *The Descent of Man, and Selection in Relation to Sex* [1871] (London: Penguin, 2004).

97 "the animal connection": Shipman, *The Animal Connection*, p. 271. Shipman also expanded on her views in personal email correspondence with the author on several occasions, including April 9, 2014; April 11, 2014; and May 24, 2014.

100 "function as if they had certain types of knowledge": Shipman, *Animal Connection*, p. 119.

104 "some scientists even suggest": Friederike Range and Zsófia Virányi, "Tracking the Evolutionary Origins of Dog-Human Cooperation: The 'Canine Cooperation Hypothesis,'" *Frontiers in Psychology* 51, no. 1582 (2015): 1–10.

108 "another likely factor": L. David Mech, "Who's Afraid of the Big Bad Wolf?" *Audubon*, March 1990.

110 "Wolves are like dogs": Simon Worrall, "How a Wolf Named Romeo Won Hearts in an Alaska Suburb," *National Geographic* online, news.nationalgeographic.com/2015/03/150322 -romeo-wolf-dog-animals-wildlife-alaska-ngbooktalk.

111 "The amazing thing": Ibid.

5. Written in the Genes

135 "That happened, he says": There are many, many articles in the popular and scientific press that discuss these ongoing controversies and new discoveries. Here are some that were particularly helpful in the writing of this book: Carl Zimmer, "Wolf to Dog: Scientists Agree on How, but Not Where," *New York Times,* November 14, 2013; David Grimm, "The Dawn of the Dog," *Science* 348, no. 6232 (2015): 274–79; Ewen Callaway, "Ancient Wolf Genome Pushes Back Dawn of the Dog," *Nature,* May 21, 2015.

138 "It is entirely possible that": Bradshaw, *In Defence of Dogs,* p. 52.

156 "Gazing into our dogs' brains": Gregory Berns, "Canine fMRI Reveals What Dogs Think of Humans," *Psychology Today* online, April 28, 2012, www.psychologytoday.com/blog/plus2sd/201204/canine-fmri-reveals-what-dogs-think-humans.

6. The Dog on the Couch: Canine Psychologists

185 "By looking at our dogs": Horowitz, *Inside of a Dog,* p. 14.

7. A Wolf on the Bed

207 "As Japanese researchers reported": Miho Nagasawa, et al. "Oxytocin-Gaze Positive Loop and the Coevolution of Human-Dog Bonds," *Science* 348, no. 6232 (2015): 333–36.

209 "Evolution took the easy route": Brian Handwerk, "Dog Gazes Hijack the Brain's Maternal Bonding System," *Smithsonian Magazine* online, April 16, 2015, www.smithsonianmag.com/science-nature/dog-gazes-hijack-brains-maternal-bonding-system-180955019/?no-ist.

SELECTED BIBLIOGRAPHY

Berns, Gregory. *How Dogs Love Us: A Neuroscientist and His Adopted Dog Decode the Canine Brain*. Boston: Houghton Mifflin Harcourt, 2013.

Bradshaw, John. *In Defence of Dogs*. London: Allen Lane, 2011.

Coppinger, Raymond, and Lorna Coppinger. *Dogs: A New Understanding of Canine Origin, Behavior, and Evolution*. Chicago: University of Chicago, 2002.

Derr, Mark. *A Dog's History of America: How Our Best Friend Explored, Conquered, and Settled a Continent*. New York: North Point, 2004.

———. *How the Dog Became the Dog: From Wolves to Our Best Friends*. New York: Overlook Duckworth, 2011.

Grimm, David. *Citizen Canine: Our Evolving Relationship with Cats and Dogs*. New York: Public Affairs, 2014.

Hare, Brian, and Vanessa Woods. *The Genius of Dogs: How Dogs Are Smarter Than You Think*. New York: Dutton, 2013.

Hobgood-Oster, Laura. *A Dog's History of the World: Canines and the Domestication of Humans*. Waco, Tex.: Baylor University Press, 2014.

Homans, John. *What's a Dog For? The Surprising History, Science, Philosophy, and Politics of Man's Best Friend*. New York: Penguin, 2012.

Horowitz, Alexandra. *Domestic Dog Cognition and Behavior: The Scientific Study of Canis Familiaris*. New York: Springer, 2014.

———. *Inside of a Dog: What Dogs See, Smell, and Know*. New York: Scribner, 2009.

Jans, Nick. *A Wolf Called Romeo*. Boston: Houghton Mifflin Harcourt, 2014.

Lopez, Barry Holstun. *Of Wolves and Men*. New York: Simon & Schuster, 1978.

Miklósi, Ádám. *Dog Behaviour, Evolution, and Cognition*. Oxford: Oxford University Press, 2007.

Schwartz, Marion. *A History of Dogs in the Early Americas*. New Haven, Conn.: Yale University Press, 1997.

Shipman, Pat. *The Animal Connection: A New Perspective on What Makes Us Human.* New York: Norton, 2011.

———. *The Invaders: How Humans and Their Dogs Drove Neanderthals to Extinction.* Cambridge, Mass.: Belknap Press, 2015.

Swinburne, Stephen R., and Jim Brandenburg. *Once a Wolf: How Wildlife Biologists Fought to Bring Back the Gray Wolf.* Boston: Houghton Mifflin, 1999.

Thurston, Mary Elizabeth. *The Lost History of the Canine Race: Our 15,000-Year Love Affair with Dogs.* Kansas City, Miss.: Andrews and McMeel, 1996.

Townshend, Emma. *Darwin's Dogs: How Darwin's Pets Helped Form a World-Changing Theory of Evolution.* London: Frances Lincoln, 2009.

INTERNET RESOURCES

Dog Cognition Lab at Barnard College, dogcognition.com
    Dr. Alexandra Horowitz directs this lab. Many helpful links.
Dognition, www.dognition.com
    Founded by Dr. Brian Hare, this website offers cognition and personality assessment tests and games for dogs, available for a one-time purchase or a subscription.
Duke Canine Cognition Center, www.evolutionaryanthropology.duke .edu/research/dogs
    Dr. Brian Hare, Duke University
    Links to ongoing research projects.
Family Dog Project, www.familydogproject.elte.hu
    Dr. Ádám Miklósi, Department of Ethology, Eötvös Loránd University, Budapest, Hungary
    This website has many links to research information, articles, photos, and videos.
Penn Vet Working Dog Center, www.pennvetwdc.org
    Dr. Cynthia Otto, University of Pennsylvania
    Includes links to research and training information.

PHOTO CREDITS

ACKNOWLEDGMENTS

Great thanks to Cynthia Platt, my amazing editor, who combines a most discerning editorial eye with endless patience, personal warmth, and the ability to see past an occasional missed deadline with good humor and grace. Her belief in this book, and in me as a writer, saw me through a year of multiple unexpected challenges, and I'm deeply grateful for that. Thank you so much for giving me space and time to write this book of my heart. I'm grateful, as well, to the entire talented team at Houghton Mifflin Harcourt. No author could ask for better hands to bring a book into the world.

Thanks to all the canine scientists who shared their knowledge with me, both through personal and email interviews and within the pages of their published articles and books. The scientific literature on dogs is expanding at a rapid pace, and though keeping up with it was daunting, I could never have written this book without the input of these researchers and access to their fascinating work.

To my human "pack": Laurel, small-animal vet extraordinaire, always ready to answer any and all of my dog-related questions; Erik, who, as a working artist, knows a thing or two about deadlines and about keeping faith in one's work in the face of all obstacles and doubts; and Lans, my number-one booster and best friend forever, who always believes I can write anything I set my mind to and never lets me aim for less. Thanks, guys, for cheering my every honor and success, and for not pointing out that it was taking me a really long time to finish this book!

And to the canine best friends, who have shared my life from earliest memory and have taught me everything I know about the bond between humans and dogs: Lady, Rebel, Shadow, Charlotte, Brutus, Alex, Asa, Finn — and to Saada and Junie, who share my couch right now as I write. Those two are teaching me still. Dogs' lives are heartbreakingly short, but life without them would be no kind of life for me. They give me comfort and joy every day.

INDEX

Bold page numbers refer to photos.

styles of learning and memory, *cont.*
   theory of mind, 188–93
   trusting relationships with humans, 178–79, 184–85, 216
   understanding of emotion in human voice, 157–63
   understanding of human gaze and gesture, 114–18, 125, 169–75
communication between dogs and humans. *See* dog-human relationship
convergence. *See* coevolution and convergence of dogs and humans

Darwin, Charles, **30**
   ethology premise, 168
   on human evolution, 73–79, **79**, 87–88
   natural selection theory, 28–31, **33**
Darwin, Erasmus, 32
detection dogs
   medical diagnosis, 226–27
   search and rescue, **1**, 217–20, **220**, **221**, **229**
   training of, 195, **196**, 199, 220, **221**
dog-human relationship. *See also* .career dogs; coevolution and convergence of dogs and humans
   archaeological burial discoveries, 2, 25–26, 37, 113
   artifacts of, 112–13
   bonding and trust, 178–79, 183–85, **207**, 207–9, **208**
   collaborative hunting, 3, **5**, 5–6, 9, **11**, 63–64, 106–12
   communication through gaze and gesture, 114–18, 125, 169–75
   empathy, 156–57
   health and social benefits, 206–7, 222–30, **224**
   Paleolithic footprints of human with dog, ix, 1, 10

reading of emotions, **115**, **131**, 157–63, **165**, 174, 185–86
dogs. *See also specific aspects of dogs*
   in ancient art and writings, **11**, 11–12, **13**, **14**
   diversity in size and shape, 29–30, **38**, 38–41, 126–27, **213**
   earliest American dogs, 16–18
   evolutionary descent from gray wolf, 30, 32–34, 88, 133–37
   genetic similarity to wolves, 39
   loss of indigenous American breeds, 19–21
   during Middle Ages, 13–14
   modern breeds with original genetic makeup, 18–19
   playfulness, **1**, 187, **187**, 189, **189**, **190**, **191**, **206**
   worldwide population, 8
dog science. *See also* cognition in dogs
   anthropomorphism, **165**, 185–86
   differentiation of dog and wolf skulls, 54–56, **62**
   fossil discoveries, 25–28, 36–37, **53**, 56–64, **60**, **63**
   geometric morphometrics, 230
   molecular biology and genetic studies, 133–36, 139–42
   multidiscipline investigations, 9
   neglect by scientific community, 168–69
   olfaction studies, 197
   radiocarbon dating of fossils, 56–57
   silver fox selective breeding study, **123**, 123–25, **124**
domestication of dogs. *See also* dog-human relationship
   breeding, 13, 15–16, **38**, 38–40, 80–85, **84**
   first alliance of humans and wolves, 88–90
   motivations for, 112, 118–21, **120**

Neanderthal Man
  extinction, 94–98
  fossil record of, 91–94
  genomic analysis of, 137
  hunting by, versus hunting by
        humans, 105–7, 112–13
North America
  arrival of domesticated dogs, 16–17
  destruction and recovery of wolf
        populations, 47–51
  early types of dogs, **11**, 17–19, **18**
  loss of indigenous dog breeds, 19–21
  oldest evidence of domesticated dogs,
        17

olfaction
  canine nasal anatomy and function,
        200–203, **202**
  coevolution of humans and dogs,
        194–95
  in medical diagnosis and assistance,
        226–27
  in search and rescue, 217–20
  training for specialized tasks, 195,
        196, 199, 220, **221**
  by untrained dogs, 197
Otto, Cynthia, 219–20

radiocarbon dating, 56–59
Range, Friederike, 102–3
rock art. *See* cave art

science. *See* dog science
scientific method, 68–71
Scott, John Paul, 168
search-and-rescue dogs, **1**, 217–20, **220**,
        221
service and assistance dogs, 227–28
Shipman, Pat, 96–97, 100, 106–12, 114,
        116–18
Skinner, B. F., 167, **167**
smell, sense of. *See* olfaction

stray dogs, 209–13, **211**

therapy dogs, 218
Thorndike, E. L., 167
Tomasello, Michael, 170–74
Topál, József, 180, 182–83

Virányi, Zsófia, 102–3

Wayne, Robert, 134–35, 136
wolves
  archaeological evidence of
        association with humans,
        37–42, 63–64, **99**
  coat colors, **43**
  cooperative social structure, 4–6, **6**,
        7, **41**, 89–90, 102–4, **103**
  first alliance with humans, 88–90
  genetic preadaptation for
        friendliness toward humans,
        137–38
  genetic similarity to dogs, 39
  human fear and persecution of,
        44–49, **45**, **46**, **48**, **49**
  recovery of North America
        populations, 49–51
  sociability and playfulness, **91**,
        108–11, **109**, **111**, **187**
  symbolic importance of, to humans,
        47, **99**
  transitional wolf-dogs, ix, 65–66,
        112, 138–39

Young, Larry, 209